Testing Children:
A Practitioner's Guide to the Assessment of Mental Development in Infants and Young Children

About the Author

Phyllis Preston – AFBPsS, C. Psychol (Clinical/Educational) – read Psychology at University College London with Cyril Burt then gained her postgraduate clinical training at the Maudsley Hospital, London Institute of Psychiatry with Hans Eysenck and Monte Shapiro. She has enjoyed a long career in applied psychology within a wide variety of settings: University Departments, National Health Service hospitals, Local Education Authority Psychological Services, schools and social services provisions. This has enabled her to sample most conditions of physical handicap, mental disorders, social deprivation, and of their consequent problems, and learn the therapies available to help relieve them.

Her experience has led her to view the mental field as a reactive determinant of malfunction in children (and adults), such as observed in learning, affective, and behaviour disorders often compounded by the deficits/deprivations of social inequality.

Her special interest in the very young was established early and still holds; she continues to teach the skill of assessing mental development to professionals working in the applied fields of psychology and paediatrics.

Testing Children:

A Practitioner's Guide to the Assessment of Mental Development in Infants and Young Children

By Phyllis Preston

HOGREFE

Library of Congress Cataloging in Publication

is available via the Library of Congress Marc Database under the
LC Control Number 2005933152

Library and Archives Canada Cataloguing in Publication

Preston, Phyllis

Testing children : a practitioner's guide to the assessment of mental development in infants and young children / Phyllis Preston.

Includes bibliographical references.
ISBN 0-88937-296-9

1. Children--Intelligence testing. 2. Psychometrics. I. Title.

RJ503.5.P72 2005 155.4'1393 C2005-906003-4

PUBLISHING OFFICES
USA: Hogrefe & Huber Publishers, 875 Massachusetts Avenue, 7th Floor, Cambridge, MA 02139
Phone (866) 823-4726, Fax (617) 354-6875; E-mail info@hhpub.com
EUROPE: Hogrefe & Huber Publishers, Rohnsweg 25, 37085 Göttingen, Germany
Phone +49 551 49609-0, Fax +49 551 49609-88, E-mail hh@hhpub.com

SALES & DISTRIBUTION
USA: Hogrefe & Huber Publishers, Customer Services Department,
30 Amberwood Parkway, Ashland, OH 44805
Phone (800) 228-3749, Fax (419) 281-6883, E-mail custserv@hhpub.com
EUROPE: Hogrefe & Huber Publishers, Rohnsweg 25, 37085 Göttingen, Germany
Phone +49 551 49609-0, Fax +49 551 49609-88, E-mail hh@hhpub.com

CORPORATE OFFICE
Hogrefe & Huber Publishers, Inc., 218 Main Street, Suite 485, Kirkland WA 98033

OTHER OFFICES
CANADA: Hogrefe & Huber Publishers, 1543 Bayview Avenue, Toronto, Ontario M4G 3B5
SWITZERLAND: Hogrefe & Huber Publishers, Länggass-Strasse 76, CH-3000 Bern 9

Hogrefe & Huber Publishers
Incorporated and registered in the State of Washington, USA, and in Göttingen, Lower Saxony, Germany

Printed and bound in Germany
ISBN 0-88937-296-9

Acknowledgements

For the help they so willingly offered I give my thanks to:

Wendy Lord, Principal Psychologist, The Test Agency, Oxford, UK, who as instigator and constant supporter of this project steered its progress. Her savoir faire in writing books proved valuable and valued.

Euan Hill, my life long companion, for so generously giving his time and expertise. His patient proof reading, critical contributions and surprising professional skills in producing the needed graphic illustrations have been particularly appreciated.

Lisa Bennett, Assistant Editor, Hogrefe & Huber, Germany, though distant geographically, quickly established friendly contact and skilful guidance through out the labour intensive tasks of reference listings and structuring of contents to bring the book to completion.

David Craig, my son-in-law, for suggesting the title.

Phyllis Preston

Table of Contents

Section Three: Issues in Application

Appendices

Introduction

This book, based on some 40 years of practice in the testing field, aims to help practitioners derive maximum benefit from the assessment possibilities inherent in individual norm based tests of mental development thereby enabling practitioners to achieve accurate results and reach conclusions best suited to the particular needs of the child under assessment.

Given that all tests of mental ability provide ample information and directions to facilitate their use and ensure correct recording and scoring of results, the reader may well ask why the use of such tests, which after all are simply measuring devices, needs to be restricted, and indeed why this book is necessary at all.

The answer to such questions lies in the fact that the use or application of an individual test of mental development is a more complex process than it may at first appear. It requires much more than simply following instructions. In fact it requires three very different types of task, each of which has a complexity of its own.

First there is the task of taking measurements of the developing mental process. This demands a quantification of the observed manifestations of mental abilities; a precise operation carried out according to well-defined rules. Although the mathematics is straightforward, it takes time and practice to become proficient in the interpretation of the resultant numerical values

The second task is that of managing an adult and a child in a situation of close interactive participation in order to gather the data. This can never be precisely controlled because there will always be many unpredictable variables such as the time of day, the inclusion of one or more siblings, the ambiance of the interview room, extraneous sounds, the mood of the child, etc.

The third task is that of the meaningful synthesis or merging of different kinds of result (scored results and individual perceptions of received information). Whatever the unpredictable variables inherent in the second task mentioned above are, it is important also to be aware of the interactive circuit set up between the observer and the observed in the assessment situation. Both the observer and the observed send and receive information they each mentally process in their own way. It is a situation fraught with potential misinterpretation, confusion and misunderstanding.

In the testing situation the process of evaluation demands the blending of skills, which assessors must constantly develop and refine.

This book is designed to help assessors understand the use of individual tests in a holistic context. In the service of that aim the text explores various avenues along which the user needs to travel prior to and during the process of testing. Some of these are strictly of a practical nature while others represent the theoretical basis needed to arrive at a reliable and valid personal evaluation of the mental process in a particular case.

Included in the chapters are reminders of those aspects of human psychology that are relevant to the appreciation of the aims of such tests and the psychometric knowledge needed to achieve meaningful, reliable and valid results. Various existing tests will be referred to in order to illustrate the most likely errors and pitfalls that may occur in the delivery of testing.

In summary this book aims to:

1) Provide a view of psychology essential to help users become more aware of the subjective elements of their perceptual mechanisms in the processing of received messages.
2) Identify where and how most common errors in the assessment process are likely to arise.
3) Look at channels of communication and warn of some pitfalls related to the user's observation skills.
4) Discuss ways to evaluate the observation of psychological functions.
5) Offer some basic information regarding the statistics required to quantify observations of performance/behaviour.
6) Describe ways to avoid common mistakes from lessons learned.

Section One: Theoretical Perspectives On Mental Measurement

In this section we start our journey through the world of assessment by taking a look at the wider context of human information processing; the way we as humans make judgements and arrive at our understanding of things generally. The use of objective assessment tools to aid human judgement is then addressed including a brief history of their emergence. An explanation is offered as to why the numerical test score alone cannot tell the whole story; that practitioners must understand not only what the objective measurement tells us but also what it leaves out; that some important aspects of the mental process must be incorporated into the assessment using practitioner skill and judgement. With this important point made, the section goes on to explore the meaning of mental development and more broadly the concepts of mind and thought. Finally, consideration is given to the impact of psychology on our understanding of the complex nature of mental development.

1 The Challenge of Evaluation

Making Sense of Information

In life, generally, the mental process and the making sense of received perceptions is a private enterprise. Trying to make sense of something is an individual task. Each one of us has a personal way of making sense of the world; of the meaning of what someone else is saying or doing; of the meaning of an unfamiliar sound or smell; of an intriguing situation, a rock formation, a piece of sculpture or a painting.

The "familiar" is that which has made sense, that which has been understood. The "strange" is that which has yet to be understood. Each one of us has a different "familiar" and a different "strange" according to our own personally felt experiences in life. This remains as true in the assessment situation as in everyday life.

When using an individual test of mental ability you are aiming to evaluate mental functions. Yet these are apparently of no substance; they are invisible and intangible. Mental functions or thought creating mechanisms cannot be seen directly; they can only be inferred through expressive displays of behaviour, performance and language. Because of the peculiar nature of mental activity, its study has to be carried out through observations of the individual engaged in some interactive way.

Psychologists have developed procedures to measure the observations of mental activity. Mental development, however, is exceedingly rapid in early infancy, and is specifically variable according to different areas of function, as well as being individually styled. Consequently mental development has proved particularly difficult to quantify precisely.

Everyone involved with the care and education of children will have observed mental development in the practicalities of day-to-day situations. Those observations combined with established common knowledge are the basis for our every day understanding of where a particular child is in his or her development, whether or not we make that understanding explicit. The established common knowledge is full of anecdotal evidence for the diversity exhibited by children in the way they manifest their thought processes. It is a diversity that continues to surprise, amuse, baffle and delight all concerned with the care of the very young

Knowledge derived from the particularities of personal every day experience is useful in that it helps us to make sense of the world. However, it is not scientific because it is unstructured, unreliable and never overtly or objectively tested to confirm or disprove its validity. To reach a more precise and empirically valid understanding of the developing mechanisms of thought requires a systematic and controlled approach. It requires the application of scientific methodology of an epistemological order; something which Jean Piaget (see reference section) began.

A Brief History of Mental Measurement

Modern psychologists, adopting scientific methodology, have applied themselves to unravelling the mystery surrounding the human mental process itself. In an attempt to find out how our mind functions, they have gathered an abundance of information on learning and the acquisition of knowledge. Spearman (1904) found a general factor underlying all activities of the mental process, which he called "g" for general intelligence. This so called factor of general intelligence, which is common to all thinking activities to a greater or lesser degree, was established by a mathematical process known as factor analysis, a method still in use today.

Psychologists developed psychometric tests that could yield a quantifiable measure of "g" (the factor of general intelligence) and thereby allow a numerical value to be assigned to mental development. The scores obtained from psychometric tests permitted results obtained from different samples to be compared and the findings tested out and reapplied repeatedly with some degree of confidence.

Over time, the notion of just one general factor of intelligence has been challenged. More recently, psychologists such as H. Gardner have introduced the notion of multiple types of intelligence, and this is reflected in the structure of tests that offer verbal, nonverbal and practical measures of mental development (e.g., Gardiner, 1993).

.As early as 1905, a French psychologist named Alfred Binet managed to achieve a numerical index of mental ability. In response to the needs of schools to identify children of very low abilities unable to learn in a large classroom situation, Binet designed a test to measure the ability to learn basic educational and reasoning skills (Binet, 1905). He devised the intelligence quotient (IQ) test, which covered a wide age range: from 3 to 16 years, and produced a quantified measure of "General Intelligence" stated in numerical terms and understood to represent the calculated level of the overall mental ability associated with scholastic skills in an individual child in the age range mentioned above.

The Binet Test (called an individual test because it is individually conducted in a one-to-one interactive situation) was translated for use in America in 1916 by an American psychologist named L. Stanford and later adapted for use in England by T. Merrill, where it became a standard psychological tool helping psychologists and educators to monitor and plan children's educational programmes and resolve individual scholastic, social and personal problems.

In the UK, the instrument became an essential tool among medical practitioners in community health, who, after receiving training as users, could perform their task of identifying children deemed "uneducable" with a greater degree of competence and reliability. Prior to such psychometric advances, children suspected of retarded development were excluded from the education system and denied schooling. It was, therefore, the task of the medical practitioner in community health to verify the condition of "uneducable" in the young pre-school aged child, as it was the responsibility of the health service to provide training centres where those so labelled could be looked after until they became of adult age. The aim of the centres was to attempt to equip the "uneducable" population with basic skills of self-management, which would give them a certain degree of independence as adults within the community.

This pejorative categorisation of children with learning difficulties was eventually remedied in 1970 with the introduction of the Education Act. The act pronounced all children, whatever their age, degree and/or type of disability, to be the responsibility of local education authorities. So, thankfully, the unfortunate historic labelling was automatically removed. This epoch making event was brought about by the accrued knowledge of psychological evidence on mental development from the pioneering works of psychologists such as Alan and Ann Clarke (e.g., 1973), and from growing strong public pressure.

Originally, because mental ability is so closely connected with language, numeracy and literacy, and is accessed for psychometric investigation through verbal forms, the study of mental development tended to start only after the occurrence of language ability: after the age of 2+ years and through into old age.

Consequently, most of the tests designed for children ignored the first two years of life. Early studies of infancy, such as those of Gesell (1925) in America, revealing though they were of the wealth and diversity of the mental process in infancy, did not constitute a developmental test of mental ability but rather observed various stages of development in the young infant. Jean Piaget's (1936, 1937) studies of mental development in children provided a rich source of material regarding the developmental stages of thought processes in children. None of these early studies, however, provided standardised measurements. These were achieved in the UK by a psychologist named Ruth Griffiths when she completed her observational study of infants from 0–2 years in 1949, and published her comprehensive findings in the form of a standardised scale of mental abilities (Griffiths, 1954).

What Test Scores Do not Measure

Although standardised tests of mental development provide a quantified score, the human mind displays, in its state of awareness (consciousness), aspects that go beyond what the numerical score from a standardised test can indicate. These aspects may be defined as follows:

a) **Attention:** that element of an individual mental process that results in the targeting at a particular point in time of something present in awareness, either internally in the mental domain or externally in the physical domain. The received stimulus may be an object, an event, a sound, an image, a smell or even a thought.

b) **Intention:** that element of the mental process that initiates activities in relation to the targeted stimulus. It includes motivation towards a thought, an object, a sound, a feeling, a situation or whatever is held in attention. It translates into ordered activities, for example, to attain a goal, secure an object to possess, disentangle a puzzle, resolve or further explore a situation.

c) **Extension:** the manner in which the targeted object is explored or investigated. That element of an individual mental process that sustains

> and develops the activities related to an intention to the full extent of the mental process of exploration and investigation, or only partially so, according to individual disposition.

It is the style and the strength or weakness of these three qualities which characterise the understanding of the individually felt experience and which contribute to the development of the mental processing system itself.

These qualities may be observed and descriptively conveyed in language using adjectives like "good," "fleeting," "poor." These in turn can be numerically graded using a point scale, such as a 4 or 6 point scale, applied to the descriptive terminology of a continuum of dichotomies such as "good/poor," "strong/weak" "sustained/fleeting," "controlled/haphazard" to obtain a numerical rating. Such descriptive grading, though assigned a numerical value, remains subjective, based on variable and discrete samples and is not precise enough to incorporate in the psychometric data of mental ability.

It is important to remember what the psychometric score ignores when it gives us a measure of mental ability in an individual child, because the unmeasured aspects are, nevertheless, an integral part of the thinking mechanism and of how the assessor understands where the child is in the development process. Psychometric tests of mental ability provide us with only partial information regarding an individual case. As test-users, if we are to maximise our understanding of the child, we must interpret what the psychometric score tells us in the wider context of the child as a whole at a point in time within a specific environment.

The key to shaping a holistic understanding of an individual child lies in the perceptions of the user. The value the user's perception contributes to the process of assessment depends on the degree of objectivity possible in skills of observation and in the styles of mental processing. When applying an individual test of mental development, the final evaluation of the findings rests squarely on the objective qualities of perception in the test-user. Test-users must ensure that their final evaluation of results is derived from both an impartial and skilled observation of the total situation and of the reliable assignment of numerical values of the scores obtained from the test used.

Points for Reflection

The use of mental tests, which after all are very finely crafted, is something that needs to be precisely taught and must necessarily remain restricted to the specifically trained professionals in the field.

In practice, the value added by any psychological test depends not only on how well the test is designed and standardised, but also how expertly the findings are evaluated. Since testing is used to help resolve a problem or a doubt regarding the developmental abilities in the individual case, it becomes all the more important that psychological tests should be appropriately handled, correctly applied, and wisely interpreted.

Psychological tests are scientifically designed and administered according to standardised procedures. The skills and suitability of the users of such tests, however, are not so rigidly examined, but the skills of the user are just as important as the tests with which the user is entrusted.

2 The Concept of Mind

An Evolutionary View

The study of the human mental process is the only area of research where the inquisitive human mind examines itself. It is something like asking a closed circuit system to investigate itself in order to understand how it functions. But, this is precisely what we humans, each one of us a dynamic, self-contained and self-adjusting living organism, have been doing all along.

When we seek to understand the dynamics of the human mental process, we cannot ignore the evidence of its collective activities across time. History provides us with a kind of mirrored global image of the evolving human mind; of its attempt to identify the mental aspects of life; to explain the ways and functions of these aspects then finally to assign to them a numerical dimension. Now that we can view mental functions with the benefit of accrued knowledge and increased experience, it seems relevant to take a backward glance, a retrospective overview of how we have got to where we are now.

From the dawn of time evidence of life is found preserved all over our world. Skeletal remains buried in sands, frozen in fields of ice, imprinted in old riverbeds, fossilised in rocks. From the tips of mountains to the deep fathomed ocean beds animal life has left enduring remains. These fragments of forms and textures have fascinated humankind. Driven by curiosity we have repeatedly applied ourselves to making sense of these mystifying vestiges. Over generations of investigative research and new finds of complete specimens, representations of what early life forms and their living experiences might have been like have become possible.

With imagination and the help of advanced technologies, the reconstruction of primitive life has been so vividly reproduced in the form of a virtual reality as to impel belief. Nowadays, experiences of the activities of dinosaurs, tigers, eagles and humans occupy a confused mix of realities in our mind.

The Mental Legacy

All of animal life leaves a legacy of traces, but human life leaves behind something more, something not contained in its remains. Humans leave behind evidence of interactive activities, interventions and manipulations of the environment and all within it; products of imagination and of creative skills, which have transformed both the human and his habitat.

From earliest time, evidence of these abilities endures in the world of realities: visible and tangible artefacts in abundance; paintings, tools, clothing, ornaments and buildings. Also in evidence is the legacy of organised living, husbandry and farming, together with continued oral communication skills individually passed on and retained in memory; story telling as legends and myths, information as to the healing or poisonous nature of plants; the production of music. Later expressive thought is transmitted visually through writing, printing, photography, which have all made for a greater exchange of thoughts. Now with electronics, exchange of thoughts is not only almost immediately possible across space, but also easily stored across time as well. Advanced technology permits realistic representations of every aspect of human activity to be preserved intact for the future.

Many human displays of variable abilities, which leave no traces in skeletal remains, and therefore appear to transcend death, continuously transform the face of the whole earth and the nature of all life on it. Nowadays, we accept these human displays as the realities of a thought process.

Because thinking appears to have no visible sensory receptors, such as the eye or the ear or the mouth to associate it with the physiology of bodily processes, such as eating, breathing and reproducing, it cannot be assigned attributes of substance and dimension. Although thinking cannot be seen, touched or tasted, the individual is aware of having thoughts but not always of how the thinking is conducted.

Soul, Mind and Thought

Thought is considered to be in the mental domain of the individual mind. Whatever the nature of this domain, the human being has demonstrated the ability to access or generate thought and convert thinking into expressed behaviour, performance and language. This invisible domain, which defies death, seemed as awesome to early man as the first flame. It inspired respect and raised fears. Of course, it awoke curiosity, the desire to understand it and the wish to bring it under control.

It is not surprising that the human invented rites and rituals, and the observation of rules, to control this apparently individually contained mysterious "spirit." This spirit was variably seen as residing in a tree, a star, a stone, a scroll, an idol, and later, to be contained within the human as a "soul." The soul was first held to reside in different parts of the human organism; in the heart or the gut, but strangely enough never in the brain. It was believed that this soul could be nurtured so as to direct its release into eternity to the advantage of its host; an appealing belief for the individual and one which is still held by and continues to sustain a great many humans to this day.

Later, however, this mysterious spirit contained in the "mind," something in the mental domain separate from the material domain of the physical body, is considered an entity imbued with feeling and thinking, specific to humans, and associated with the function of the individual human brain. It established the awareness of individual existence, famously expressed by Descartes's statement "Je pense donc je suis" (I think therefore I am). It did not take long for a body/mind dichotomy to ensue and for the mind to become a field of study in its own right.

Body and Mind

At first, the nature of mind was a concern in the realm of philosophy, as it studied the nature of thought. Then psychology took over and applied itself to the study of the thinking process itself and identified its various sequential levels as a logical reasoning progression, and later managed to achieve a way to measure its development.

Currently science (including neurology, nuclear physics, psychology, psycholinguistics, physiology, biochemistry, biology) has taken over the task of understanding the mind through the study of the human brain in function, and the mental domain has once more re-entered the material domain of the human body.

Thanks to technological advances the neurosciences have made impressive discoveries about the brain's electric pathways. The human brain has been minutely studied in live function and caught in vision; clearly visible neurons firing pulses, unfolding waves, establishing specific pathways and global electric fields. The biochemists have identified chemicals critical to the maintenance of neural synaptic activities in the brain's changing wiring systems. Their collective findings have seen the emergence of theories such as that of the "embodied mind" (Varela, Thompson & Rosch, 1992) and the "mindful brain," (Edelman & Mountcastle, 1978; Freeman, 1999), some of which would reduce mental functions to physiological data.

Unfortunately, all these new theories ignore the environment as an essential interactive variable, which structures both physical and mental abilities. They also ignore the as yet un-revealed link between information derived through the sensory receptors and proprioceptors, with their neural electric pathways clearly chartered in the brain, and the information derived from the individually perceived felt experience with, as yet, unidentified pathway representations in the brain. Also unexplained is the thorny matter of personal choice and the neglected or dismissed phenomena of pre-cognition, of telepathy, of meta-cognition and of morphogenetic fields (Sheldrake, 2003).

Despite the impressive achievements of the neurosciences, the nature of the mental processing system still remains something private. The body/mind status may now be accepted by some as no longer dichotomous, but interdependent in some ways not yet fully understood. However, the duality of a body and a mind – a Cartesian inheritance – persists, and the inquisitive mind keeps on searching.

3 The Psychological Route

Issues in Communication

The individual can communicate through a variety of ways such as facial expressions: a way of looking, grimacing; through body movement: a gesture, a stance. But it is language that remains the main channel of communication, because language is the expressive representation of thought. Whether expressed through the modality of vision (as in drawing and writing) or vocally through speech/singing, it facilitates the exchange of ideas, of information, and increases knowledge.

Without language, communication would be restricted and cumbersome and mental ability less well developed. Having a common language makes verbal communication easy and meaningful. Without a common language between people, conversation becomes very limited and frustrating if not just impossible.

Similarly professionals in specialised fields, such as the different branches of science, medicine, or psychology, have their own language and concepts. They can communicate easily within their own fields for they share a common vocabulary and common concepts for their specific terms. But when they wish to engage in an exchange of information across their particular professional fields they need the help of translators and interpreters to understand one another and meaningfully advance their knowledge.

Using an individual psychological test of mental development presupposes a professional foundation in the psychological aspects of mental ability and the ways in which it is evaluated. It presupposes knowledge of the language used in psychology.

For all users who may not be familiar with or who may not have had a foundation in those aspects of psychology relevant to mental testing, the information provided in this chapter may offer a useful synopsis.

Nowadays some areas of psychology are established as a science and as such are restricted to scientific methodology, which depends on assigning numerical values to derive a psychological measurement. As yet, mental function, and its development, does not lend itself completely to the scientific methodology of psychological measurement because it remains rooted in the individual awareness of the perceptual mechanism of the felt experience, which is of a qualitative nature.

The qualitative aspect of the mental thought process poses a different kind of problem to that of assigning a numerical value. Making sense of a personal felt experience introduces the element of subjectivity. Mental development and the mental process itself appear to be individually crafted.

Two Different Faces of Psychology

Romanishyn (1982) makes a distinction between, on the one hand, modern psychology as a science with its basis in the physics of the world and the physiology of the body, and, on the other hand, psychology as a personal life experience, and expands on the importance of the latter. Thus, as he suggests, psychology has two faces, which makes for at least two different ways of understanding mental development.

It would seem appropriate to consider, very briefly, the difference between these two faces of psychology. An understanding of the distinction is pertinent to users of individual tests for the assessment of mental development in children because assessors must be aware that to be scientific they must step back from their anecdotal or subjective experiences of the psychological processes. The elements of the two faces of psychology are summarised as follows:

Psychology as a Science	**Psychology as a Personal Life Experience**
1. Relies on strict methodology	1. Depends on the perception of individually felt experiences
2. Requires precise measurements	2. Based on emotions – metaphors – hunches
3. Sets levels of significance and rejection criteria	3. Accepts beliefs – common sense – uncorroborated stories – is individualistic – seemingly unconcerned with verification.

4. Is in the public domain – opened to challenge – inspection	4. Covert – private – personal – secret
5. Enables the definition of mental functions in terms of variables which are arithmetically measurable in terms of time – size – clustering – spread	5. Shapes reality into personal (virtual) realities influences human function – creates drives – desires – liable to confusion & ambiguity: difficult to define or measure
6. Deals with the sensory received elements from the outside world and the internal body sensations	6. Refers to perceived (personal) mental/emotional elements revealed out of choice in expressed forms of performance, behaviour, language

Gateways to the Mental Domain

Various gateways to the mental domain are established through the mechanism of perception, which, in turn, is dependent on the receptive channels, of which touch, sight, sound, smell and taste are perhaps the more obvious ones. This dependence on sensory input is open to errors in transmission. Sometimes our receptors are impaired or their transmitting channels damaged. They could distort, misinform or only partially inform our perception. Also our perception can be so tricked by emotions, beliefs, bias, false expectations and illusions as to ignore or distort the sensorially received information. In addition, perception is vulnerable to the fallibility of memory.

Given this somewhat fanciful relationship between reception and perception it is not surprising to find that, in our everyday psychological life, we accept ambiguity and confusion; in fact we often ignore them. However, if assessors are to develop their skills of observation, it is important that they understand and remain aware of the tricks our minds can play.

Some of these can best be illustrated as follows:

a) Visual Illusions

Table 1 illustrates the following visual illusions:

Table 1. Visual Illusions

i

ii

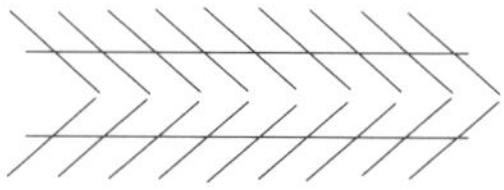

iii

iv

In i), we see two lines and easily judge one being longer than the other, but they are both of the same length.

In (ii), parallel lines that do not appear parallel.

In (iii), the Ponzo model, we see a triangle that is not in fact there, and science dismisses this "visual perception" as an illusion, a vision within our mind and not in the reality of the world. Yet we see a triangular shape, in the mental domain and we may also perceive it as setting up a parameter of forces with psychological implications of relationship.

In (iv), the figure ground phenomenon demonstrates a characteristic human tendency to alternate seeing a shape in its background with seeing the background as a shape. This is known as figure ground reversal.

A famous psychological theory, known as the "Gestalt" (see, for example Koffka, 1935) established the perceptual tendency to re-arrange the sensory input of closely placed similar shapes and unfinished familiar patterns by automatically grouping the shapes and completing the familiar incomplete image as received realities. The artist Salvador Dali surprises and bemuses us with his artistic visual illusions of figure ground reversals, embedded images, three dimensional effects and seemingly impossible representations.

In the testing situation, it is not uncommon to observe that when young children are asked to copy a large square divided by two lines into four inner squares they draw just four separate small squares. This could reflect a figure ground reversal phenomenon, the large square often referred to as a "window" (the figure: a window and its four panes), while the four small squares suggest the panes (the ground). Also, during the monitoring of the testing interview, the assessor's focus of attention alternates between the child (the figure) and the accompanying adult/s (the ground) to take in any changes (of mood, attitude and behaviour) in either or both.

b) Language Illusions:

Language is a rich source of conflict in the individual; the intended meaning of what is transmitted isn't always the same as the meaning attributed to what is received. The use of metaphors illustrates this situation. As an example, we know that in 1666 Newton, experimenting with light, passed a ray of sunlight (known as white light) through a prism. It broke up into a spectrum the colours of the rainbow. He had discovered that white light is made up of the colours of the rainbow and for him, light spectrum and rainbow are one and the same. However, the psychological experience of looking at a rainbow allows a differentiation. Looking at a rainbow in the sky arouses emotions. To most of us it is a beautifully coloured arc across the sky. To the poet Keats (1884) it was a woven cloth.

He expressed this as follows:

> There was an awful rainbow once in heaven:
> We know her wool, her texture, she is given
> In the dull catalogue of common things
> Philosophy will clip an Angel's wings
> Conquer all mysteries by rule and line
> Empty the haunted air, and gnomed mine
> Unweave a rainbow

Despite his knowledge of the physics of a rainbow, looking at a rainbow remains, for the poet and for most of us, an emotive personal felt experience. In order to communicate this experience, Keats used a metaphor. The metaphor is a way of seeing one reality through another. If you know what a woven cloth looks like, you too can see the rainbow as a piece of woven cloth. To understand a metaphor one has to participate in the vision of the mental domain and to do so one has to have a common basis in language.

This practice of substituting words happens simply because all language is a way of transmitting meaning, and, therefore, all language is potentially metaphorical. We can never be sure that a message we send out is the message the listener receives. This is why sometimes when we wish to convey an unusual idea, or a daring plan for some undertaking, we tend to begin by saying "Imagine …" then proceed with more specific details. Imagination could be said to be a natural characteristic of the mind which helps the individual perceptions of received sensory information to be refigured in a variety of different ways. We need imagination to enter into the reality of a vision perceived through someone else's mental experience as expressed in language and to be able to participate in its vision. In other words, we need imagination to be able to reach common understanding.

This has important consequences for the assessor conversing with a child or the parent of that child. In the shared understanding of conversational meaning, there is a degree of what is called "intersubjectivity." The extent of shared understanding depends on the degree of the participants intersubjectivity. In conversation, we tend to overestimate the degree of intersubjectivity that exists; we tend to assume equal understanding of language use. There are specific dangers relating to allowing such an assumption in the assessment context. Thus, consider the following example:

During an interview the parent tells the assessor that the child is "bright." The word bright means different things to different people. It may refer to a manner of behaviour: a happy, out-going child; or one delighting in physical activities; or a quiet undemanding child content to pursue self engendered tasks. It may refer to academic achievements: a child who does well at school. It may refer to a child with creative ability; inventive; or with having a specific ability pursued almost obsessively. If the assessor's understanding of the word bright is different from that of the parent's, and if the assessor does not check this out, then already an error has occurred.

c) Mental Illusions: Beliefs

Belief is perhaps best illustrated by considering the mirror image: the reflected. We are familiar with the mirror image and accept the scientific explanation of how a reflection is produced by the deflection of light rays.

The image and the viewer appear equidistant from the surface of the mirror but in the opposite direction and laterally reversed. Although we know that the image lies on the surface of the mirror, when we view the reflection we do not see the mirror. Photographers are often puzzled by the fact that the lens must be focussed not at the distance of the mirror but at the perceived distance of the reflected object in order to capture the image correctly in focus. The mirror, as an object in reality, has disappeared or become part of the lens system.

The perceived distance is an illusion, and the image is a virtual image of no substance. Yet as a felt experience it is perceived as having a dimension of reality and one with which we communicate. The communication appears reciprocal. The reflection arouses the mental process into interactive investigation to understand the other reality and make use of it.

When we look at our image we do not appear to be put off by the reversed laterality. The image we see matches the kinaesthetic appreciation of our body. Thus we make faces in the mirror to see the look of the reflected image restructured in different ways; the ballet dancer uses the mirror to perfect a movement even though when lifting a right arm, for example, the mirror image in vision is positioned as a left arm; similarly for the actor who looks at a mirror to study stance and facial expression to better his performance. But, try and trace a star pattern by looking only at its mirror image and you have to adjust to the problem of reversed laterality.

The interaction between the perception of a virtual image and a reality creates a felt experience of confusion, which may be considered a positive phenomenon because what happens when we look at our reflected image creates a belief; a belief in the virtual image as a reality that we have restructured and that matters. We also reinforce a belief that "I see things because I am also visible – and the reverse, leading to the conclusion that "if I can't see I am invisible." Very young children when first introduced to hide and seek games tend to cover up their faces. They thus demonstrate their belief that if they can't see then they cannot be seen. Experience teaches us otherwise, but the mechanism that creates belief remains.

One of the test items used in the assessment of mental development in infants is a mirror presented so as to reflect the infant's face full on. The infant responds by looking, smiling at and patting the mirror image, and frequently by kissing the image. The infant behaves as if the image is an object in reality. Sometimes the infant looks behind or turns the mirror over as if searching for a "real" face or person, thus reinforcing the impression that at the early stages of perceptual development the infant does not distinguish between the virtual and the real, but treats all visual perceptions as realities.

Underlying Processes in the Mental Domain

Psychology deals with the intricate nature of human mental activities. The mental process manipulates personally felt experiences. Mental activity is a process that transforms "substance": the visible, tangible realities of the world we live in into an invisible experience in our individual inner world.

People can choose to make this private experience overt (visible) through the various channels of expression, such as language written or spoken, including the use of metaphors and beliefs, or by gesturing and body stances. In other words, we communicate our felt experiences by placing them back as realities of the world we live in, and, as such, they can be received through the sensory channels and then individually understood through the mechanism of perception. In this way, interactive communication, with all its implications for errors and misunderstandings as well as for development and learning, takes place.

Any training course set up to teach the use of a psychological test to evaluate the mental development of infants and young children needs to ensure that the trainees have acquired an appreciation of the elements of psychological growth.

Before plunging into the practicality of administrative test procedures, the trainee should have some understanding of the progressive nature of the thinking process, which can be identified in hierarchical stages of mental development, but which do not follow precisely a chronological order.

The Structure of Thinking (see also Appendix 1)

There seems to be a natural progression in the development of the mental process that is reflected in the outward displays of behaviour, language and skills of the growing child. This mental progression can be observed in the expressions of performance, behaviour and language. By studying these expressions of mental activities psychology has derived some understanding of the underlying structure, or "constructs," of the thought process and the formation of "concepts." All individual tests of mental development contain a series of graded tasks that tap the structure of the thinking process. The assessor has to present these tasks and record the successes and failures.

For example, if we ask a child to sort out different shapes, or coloured chips, or different sizes of one specific shape, the way he tackles the task will tell us whether he understands the concepts of "same" and "different" and of using the construct of categories to do the sorting task.

If we ask a child to complete a given number sequence and she completes it correctly, she has demonstrated deductive thinking (the manipulation of concepts to arrive at a hypothesis and make a prediction, which is considered to be at a more advanced level than the mental process displayed in the first example).

Of course, we can see thinking processes being demonstrated outside the context of psychometric testing. Television quiz shows are a good example. A television quiz show host might ask contestants to look at four photographic portraits then name "the odd one out" or the reverse. The contestants are asked to look at apparently unrelated objects/pictures and state "the common link." Success here depends on knowledge of the objects/pictures presented, and the ability to abstract a common thread. In order to achieve this, the contestants must be able to access (retrieve) what they have stored in memory from knowledge accrued from past experiences.

Thinking progresses from the ability to achieve rational logic from a concrete level to an abstract level, which is demonstrable in the ability to identify, sort, group, make categories, extract a common factor, deduce a relationship, formulate a hypothesis (make a kind of prediction and test it out), formulate and manipulate abstract concepts; all in order to come to understand the truth of the matter.

In parallel with the development of rational logic, there appears to be an early appreciation of space, derived through the manipulation of objects and the observation of objects in motion, which leads to the awareness of causality and the constructs of time and of speed. If the question "which goes faster an aeroplane flying or a bird flying?" is put to a 3-year-old child the most likely answer is "a bird flying." The young child experiences the direct reception of the relatively fast speed at which a bird flies across his/her field of vision to quickly disappear, while the aeroplane remains much longer in view before vanishing away. At this stage s/he responds to sensed reception without the application of logical reasoning, nor as yet the abstract understanding of speed as a construct.

All the while there is a mechanism of retention and recall that stores and retrieves information as required and which is called memory. There is long-term memory, which can be recalled over a very long period of time, and short-term memory, which is more immediate in recall, such as information crammed in haste to pass an exam and is then mostly forgotten soon after. Whatever its type and its intricate nature, memory plays a key role in the learning process of coming to know the realities of the world and of constructing an individual identity.

Objective tests contain tasks designed to assess aspects of the thinking process and it is, of course, crucial for the assessor to understand how the task relates to the construct being measured. This knowledge must be blended with skilled observation, which helps the assessor to more readily spot any unusual pattern of failures that may be significant because it does not follow the stages of the thinking process, or an intriguing success/failure that may need further information or verification as it may reveal an error or indicate a specific strength or a specific weakness in the thinking process.

But the assessor must do more than simply focus on the task, because there is another aspect of thinking that cannot be objectively tested: it relates to individual choice and decision making. The decision-making element is always present, enabling the child to make a choice about whether to express the outcome of a thought process overtly (verbally, by performing a task, making gestures, nodding, smiling, etc.) or to refrain and keep the outcome private (which is called covert).

The use of individual choice applies right through the interactive process of learning from the very start. We choose to look at one particular object out of many. We choose to listen to one sound and ignore others. We choose to either keep our thoughts secret or divulge them. In our interactions we choose to either intervene or refrain from so doing. What determines individual choice remains a puzzle as the act of choice appears, sometimes, to be idiosyncratic; it is not always the product of reason, or emotions alone, and it is not always of apparent benefit to the individual concerned.

During the assessment process, the assessor uses his or her own logical thinking processes to arrive at hypotheses about the behaviour of the child. For example, if a child is un-cooperative (remaining silent or refusing to tackle tasks), the assessor must form a hypothesis about the reason for this. It could be due to any number of reasons such as:

- shyness;
- over cautiousness;
- the inability to cope with a new task without guidance;
- a fear of failure which reveals a weakness/incapacity to perform the demanded task, thus endangering the self image of competency;
- a strong ego, s/he likes to control a situation, or remain in charge of the situation;
- a high degree of immaturity; or
- a perceptual deficit, unable to participate, detached or oblivious of the interactive nature of life

A skilled assessor derives information from observations of the child from the very start of the interactive interview and so can interpret the cause of the non-co-operation more correctly. The skilled observer, being aware of the alternative hypotheses as to what is causing the behaviour, is able to judge the best approach to gain co-operation rather than act on a trial and error basis or just automatically administer the test without taking account of the child's reactions.

In summary, then, for effective assessment the assessor must:

- understand the mental development process;
- be clear about how the constructs measured by tests relate to the structure of thinking;
- have enough knowledge of psychometrics to be able to interpret the numerical scores derived from tests;
- effectively manage the interpersonal dynamics of the assessment process;
- have highly developed skills of observation; and
- be adept at merging all of the above skills to form clear and valid conclusions that lead to action that is in the best interests of the child under assessment.

The remaining sections of this book aim to help practitioners to develop these crucial skills.

Section Two: A Guide to Psychometrics

In this section, Chapter 4 explains in down to earth terms the essential statistics required to interpret test scores. Appendix notes 2, 3 and 4 provide more specific information regarding the nature and function of measurements, the normal distribution curve and its relation to IQ values. Chapter 5 presents an overview of tests of mental ability.

4 About Numerical Values of Mental Ability

The Meaning of Numbers

Scores on tests are numerical values. The first important thing to understand about test scores is that, whatever the particular test of mental development used, the resultant numerical value represents a *relative* position. It does not indicate a dimension of absolute size. Psychological measurement differs in this sense from physical measurement. Consider these examples:

a) Physical Measurement (Arithmetical Ratio Scales)

If a table is measured as being five metres long and another table is measured as being ten metres long, then we can say that one table is twice the size of the other.

b) Psychological Measurement (Arithmetical Interval Scales)

If a child gets a test score of five and another child gets a test score of ten, we cannot say that one child has twice the ability of the other.

The key difference between physical and psychological measuring scales is that the latter do not start from a zero value. The starting point for psychological measuring scales is some sort of expected standard against which an individual is measured. The most common standard for assessing mental development in children is the typical level of performance in "most" children of a certain age. The psychological starting, or zero point, is set at this "most" value. Thus, if we expect most children to get a score of between ten and twelve, the scores obtained by individual children will be compared to this expected standard. If a child scores eight, then clearly that child is below the expected standard, but how far below? What is the significance of two or three or four points below the expected standard? In order to answer these questions, it is necessary to understand more about the nature of psychological measurement.

Norm-Referenced Testing

The numerical value derived from a psychological test simply tells us how a specific child stands in relation to a peer group; how close the child's score is to the majority that occupy a central position (the average) in the group, or how far away it is from the level at which the majority score.

In other words, the numerical value is a measure of *how much* the score deviates from the achieved average range of the sampled group. The sampled group are referred to as the *norm group*.

The norm group is the standard or benchmark against which we compare the performance of an individual child. The choice of norm group is therefore crucial. The norm group must be selected to be representative of whatever category of children we wish to compare the individual child against. For example, if we wish to compare the individual against all children in the UK, then our norm group must include the same range of variables that categorise all children in the UK in a similar percentage to that which exists in the total population. Variables might include age of child, education level of parent, ethnic group and many others.

Understanding how the norm group performs on a test is a key part of the development of the test as well as key to subsequent interpretations of the test in practice.

A well-constructed test must be appropriate in difficulty level and content for whatever section of the population it is designed to assess. If the test is appropriate in difficulty and content for the norm group chosen, then we expect that the average score for the group will be around 50% of the highest possible score. We would expect most of the sample to score at or close to the average score for the group. Fewer and fewer children will score further and further from the average. When this distribution of scores is plotted on a graph, the resulting curve will be a symmetrical bell shape. Since this is how we normally expect the scores of the sample group to be distributed, the curve is referred to as the *normal dis-*

tribution. In order to be able to interpret a numerical score derived from a test, it is important to understand the concept of the normal distribution as well as other statistical concepts.

Nowadays, references to statistics are regularly made in the public domain to inform us of practically every aspect of life: financial, commercial, social, political. Bar graphs, distribution curves, percentile ranks, are familiar sights not only in scientific journals but also on advertising posters. They are used (or misused) convincingly for the promotion of a product or the justification of an idea. However, unless versed in the way the findings are derived the presented information may prove misleading or meaningless.

Because the psychometric structure of mental tests uses specific statistical concepts and terminology, there is the need to establish a common basis of knowledge as to the nature of this statistical language. Most tests of mental development explain the mathematics of the statistics of their construction and there are many books on the statistics used in psychology. Because statistics is part of the language of mathematics, which uses concepts of numbers, signs and symbols in a variety of specific ways, it is not always easy to understand.

What Do We Need to Know?

a) How Mental Ability Normally Develops Across the Life-Span

Mental ability is a natural human characteristic that develops over time. Consequently, its measured values should be, to some extent, age-related in a continuum from birth to maturity and, therefore, should be capable of being documented. In the area of early childhood, which extends from 0 to 8 years, mental development is rapid and variable. In this age range, the nature of mental development measured as a continuum has been very nearly achieved but not quite.

b) The Unit of Measurement to Be Used

Every measurement requires a unit of measure and a scale to grade the measured values. We need to know something about the unit of measurement and about the nature of the scale. Scales have to be reliable standards, like the metre or the thermometer, so that measurements can be trusted in their application for comparison over time, place and sampled groups.

c) The Degree of Error in our Measurement

All measurements carry an error and we need to know the size of this error of measurement since it indicates the implicit variations specific to the measurement. Simply put, the score a child achieves on an ability test can only ever be an estimate of the child's true ability. There will always be some error of measurement. It is important to quantify the likely size of the error. For example, if on one testing occasion the child scores say 15 on a test and we know that the error of measurement is two score points, then we can confidently say that the child's actual level of ability is somewhere between 13 and 17. So knowing the error in the measurement allows us to be aware of a possible minimum and maximum value for a recorded measurement; in other words, it indicates an expected range of values according to the error of the particular measurement.

d) How the Unit of Measurement Chosen Relates to the Normal Distribution

In order to understand the numerical dimension of mental development, we need to know how the unit of measurement is derived and what has determined the nature of the measuring scale adopted.

e) How the Score Relates to Mental Age

We need to know the appropriate mathematics used; why all the scores achieved on a test of mental development are translated into months and years, or, as in the case of very young infants, generally calculated in weeks and months; what these are taken to represent; and how they become translated into a standard score.

The Concept of Mental Age

Because mental ability appears to progress over time it is measured in relation to chronological age. The measured ability can be translated into an Equivalent Mental Age (MA). One way of expressing how mental age relates to chronological age is to divide Mental Age by the child's Chronological Age (CA), also expressed in weeks/months/years, and multiply the result by 100 (to avoid a decimal point and round off to a whole number). When MA = CA, the resultant quotient ([MA/CA] × 100) = 100, and is taken to indicate the average mental ability level and seems to have been chosen as the conventional zero point value setting for all norm-based scales of mental development.

Depending on how a test is constructed, the IQ (a unit of mental measurement) may represent the general level of development (extracted from a summation of all scores obtained from the test) or the specific level of development obtained from subscales that purport to measure specific areas of function such as motor MQ, verbal VQ, performance PQ, and so on. All these IQs are calculated numerical values of units of displayed mental development. What they represent, their meaning for an individual child under investigation requires some understanding of psychometric techniques.

Understanding the Nature of Psychometric Tests

A psychometric test is essentially a series of tasks or questions. Each task or question is referred to as a test item. At the most basic level, psychometric tests are instruments that assess some aspect of human behaviour – either some aspect of intellectual functioning or some aspect of behavioural style. The thing that makes psychometric tests different from other methods of assessment is not so much *what* they measure but *how* they measure it.

There are four characteristics that define the nature of psychometric measurement.

a) Objectivity and Impartiality

First and foremost, any test worthy of the label "psychometric" must provide objective measurement. Objective measurement means that the score a test-taker achieves on the test is independent of the beliefs and opinions of the person administering and interpreting it. In addition, psychometric tests should discriminate between test-takers ONLY on the basis of whatever attribute is being measured. We must be sure that neither gender nor creed nor race nor disability will impact on the score a test-taker achieves.

b) Standardisation

The next characteristic of psychometric tests is that they are standardised. Standardisation is so central to psychometric tests that sometimes people call them standardised tests instead of psychometric tests. In terms of test usage, standardisation refers to the fact that there is a standard way to administer a test and a standard way to score it. But that's not all there is to standardisation. Standardisation also forms a crucial stage in the development of a psychometric test. At the development stage, standardisation is the process of ensuring that the content and the difficulty level of the test is appropriate for whatever section of the population it is aimed at. So if the test is being designed for children, the test-developer will try it out on a large sample of children.

Once the test is published test-users must ensure that they administer the test under conditions that are as similar as possible to the conditions that existed when the test was standardised. This is because the conditions under which a test is given affect how children perform on the test. The further you deviate from the conditions under which the test was standardised, the less you can rely on the information obtained during the testing process.

There are some standard procedures that apply to all psychometric tests, but there are also some nuances of procedure that are specific to particular tests. One of the test-user's responsibilities is to read and follow the test-developer's specific instructions for administering and scoring. You will find these in the manual that accompanies the test along with all the other technical information you need to know in order to use the test. All tests should be accompanied by a test manual. If there isn't a manual, then you are strongly advised not to buy the test.

So standardisation initially occurs when the test is developed but it is also part and parcel of test usage. Standardisation is what makes a test objective and impartial.

c) Reliability – Degree of Accuracy

The third characteristic of psychometric tests is reliability. This refers to the margin of error in a test's measurement. No psychological measuring instrument can ever be 100% precise – there will always be a certain margin of error. In other words, the score a child gets on a test won't precisely reflect that child's true level of whatever is being measured. It will just be an estimate. The more reliable the test, the better the estimate will be, but it will never be 100% precise. Where psychometric tests have an advantage over other forms of assessment is in the fact that they actually specify how big the margin of error is. Reliability is quantified using an index between zero and one. The closer the reliability is to one, the more reliable the test. We normally expect tests to have a reliability of at least 0.7 to be useful.

A reliable test should show consistency and provide results that would not show great variation when the test is repeated over time. It is important to remember that scores that lie close to the mean of the sample tend to be more reliable than scores that lie at the extreme points of the frequency distribution and are distant from the mean value.

From the reliability we can calculate the expected margin of error around individual test scores.

While it is the test-developer's responsibility to establish the reliability of the test, it is the test-user's responsibility to take account of reliability when interpreting test scores.

The reliability of the user is equally important and users should develop consistency in their delivery of the test and its scoring. Unreliable tests are worthless. It has to be remembered, however, that a reliable test does not necessarily mean a good test unless it is also a valid test.

d) Validity

Where reliability concerns the precision with which a test measures something, validity, the fourth characteristic here, concerns whether the "something" the test is measuring is actually what it claims to be measuring. If, for example, a test claims to be measuring verbal reasoning, there must be evidence that it really is verbal reasoning that affects the score a child gets. Validity refers to the suitability of the test in its application to measure a specific dimension or ability. A test is valid if it measures the characteristics it was designed to measure. For example, using a metre as a unit of length to measure a length of cloth is a valid tool but it would be an invalid tool for measuring the weight of an object. Some tests may not be suitable for the purpose for which they are used; for instance using a verbal test to tap the mental ability level of a child with severe speech problems, or using paper-and-pencil tasks to evaluate the mental ability of a partially sighted child. In both instances the results would be of very low validity and unreliable.

The questions of validity and of reliability or of consistency in the test and in the user have to be kept in mind. Many factors external to the test may affect both the reliability and validity of the findings, not least of all the degree of competence and reliability of the user. Undesirable conditions in the testing situation, and in the physical or affective state of the child and of the examiner, at the time of testing, may also invalidate test results.

More About the Process of Test Development

Essentially, to standardise a test, the developer must first administer the test to a group that represents the population that the test has been designed to assess – we call them the standardisation sample. Next the test-developer has to analyse how the standardisation sample performed on the test. Then finally, the test-developer has to communicate this information.

The simplest way to look at how the standardisation sample has performed on a test is to make a chart in the form of a table or a graph to visually represent the distribution of test scores in the sample.

The first thing the test-developer will do is draw up what's called a frequency distribution. A frequency distribution is a table that shows how many children got each possible score on the test. At this stage, we can't make any interpretation of what various scores mean in terms of level of mental development. The scores are simply how many items children got correct. For this reason, they are called raw scores, because they need to be refined to make them meaningful. It is the process of standardisation that will give them meaning. But at the moment, all the test-developer has is a frequency distribution. The frequency distribution tells us whether the test is appropriate for the standardisation sample. If it is appropriate, we would hope to see some children scoring in each score band but with most children in the sample scoring somewhere around the halfway mark. If we plotted such a distribution on a graph, the curve of the graph would be in the shape of a bell. This bell-shaped curve is referred to as the "normal frequency distribution," because it is how we expect the scores of a sample to be distributed if the test used is appropriate for the population it is aimed at. The normal distribution is also sometimes referred to as the "Gaussian Curve," after the name of the mathematician who discovered its mathematical properties.

The frequency distribution of any numerical dimension assigned to the mental process, when collected in vast numbers, should form a distribution curve pattern very similar to that of the normal frequency distribution or bell-shaped curve.

Consequently, most psychological tests of mental development are designed so that the frequency distribution of their collected numerical values, called the raw data, follows as near as possible the pattern of the ideal normal frequency distribution. These types of tests are called norm-based.

By using the mathematics of the normal curve the raw scores assigned to a mental process can be converted to a standardised numerical value. The psychometric scale could be thought of as a standardised measuring tool giving readings of mental ability in standard units, something akin to a thermometer giving readings in degrees of heat. To convert raw data into a standard score requires some further arithmetical manipulation.

The normal distribution curve has the following properties:

1) Measures of centrality

The normal distribution curve informs us about the most typical or average level of performance. There are three ways to quantify this:

- The mean:
  denotes the most typical score obtained by the sample. In a normal distribution the mathematical value of the mean (average value) will be at around half the total score value.
- The median
  is the value at the exact mid point of the distribution. It dissects the range of scores in equal halves.
- The mode
  is the most frequently occurring score.

In a normal distribution the mean, median and mode will all be of equal value: mean = median = mode

This won't be the case in distributions that are skewed. For example, if a test is too difficult for most of the group, the scores are likely to be low, except for a few exceptional cases. The inclusion of these cases will distort the mean score upwards so that it will be higher than the mode with the median somewhere in between.

2) Measures of Spread

These tell us about how much variation there is in the sample's ability. Two ways of quantifying spread are described below:

- The range:
  tells us how much people in the sample vary in their performance on this test. The range is the distance from the lowest to the highest value and forms the base of the bell-shaped curve of distribution. If the test is appropriate for the population being tested, we would expect to see members of the sample scoring across the whole possible range of test scores.
- The standard deviation (*SD* or sigma, ó)
  tells us the average amount by which the scores of individuals in the sample deviate from the most typical score. Like the range it is a measure of spread, but it specifies not the total range across the whole sample but rather the range of scores that would indicate average performance. In the normal curve of frequency distribution, the average range is defined as one standard deviation either side of the mean – 68% of people are expected to occupy this average range.

IQ in Relation to the Normal Distribution Curve

The label "IQ" (Intelligence Quotient) as the measure of the mental ability value continues to be in use, but mental ability value is no longer derived from a quotient; it is a calculated standard score. In the course of standardisation, the distribution of measured mental ability values should resemble, as near as possible, that of the normal frequency distribution, with a mean set to 0 point and a *SD* of 15 points. The range of these values would then extend from the –4 *SD* to the +4 *SD* point equality spread on either side of the 0 point of its mean and, if expressed in IQs, the range would extend from approximately IQ 0.1 to IQ 164+, with its mean at IQ 100.

Standard scores enable a meaningful comparison between different standardised tests, and the calculation of significance of the difference between test scores, which is necessary to know for diagnostic purposes. They also permit equivalence scores to be established with different calculations of frequency distributions.

Some important points to bear in mind

- A child with an IQ of 60, as a measured value of mental ability, cannot be said to have half the mental ability of a child with IQ120: this comparison is meaningless. (See Appendix 3 for a model of the normal curve and its related derived values and equivalent descriptive classifications.)
- Suppose two children score an IQ of 130 on a test of mental ability. One is aged 4 years old and the other is aged 6 years. Both are well above average in their respective peer groups, but the measured display of ability of the 4 year old is not equal to that of the 6 year old. This is so because we do not have an absolute measure.
- Partly for the same reason it is also difficult to predict with certainty whether, for example, a child of 4 years will maintain, improve or even appear to lose his or her measured display of ability. The relative position within a peer group is not guaranteed over a long period of time. This is so not only because of various unpredictable variables but also because the displayed development of the mental system, unlike chronological age, is neither linear nor strictly continuous in time.
- The error of measurement (*SEM*), inherent in any form of measurement carried out by an individual using a tool, is calculable from the reliability of the test. It occurs in psychological measurements and is generally found to be a variable zone of incaccuracy on either side of an obtained score, usually between 3 to 12 points according to age and area of function measured. Infants and young children are somewhat unreliable performers and their rate of de-

velopment, while very rapid, tends to fluctuate. For this reason the adoption of a higher estimate of the error of measurement, up to +/ –5 points, is more appropriate, except in cases where a calculated *SEM* is given. It is strongly advised when quoting an IQ to add the +/– *SEM* points to account for the zone of inaccuracy and give the resulting IQ as a numerical range; thus, for example: IQ125 should be recorded as IQ 120–130 range when an *SEM* of10 points is taken into account to clearly indicate that any difference in value between the range IQ 120 and 130 should not be treated as significant. This advice applies more particularly when testing very young children for diagnostic purposes; it should certainly not be used in research.

- As already stated most psychological tests of mental ability are norm based. There are some tests which are not norm based but are criteria based, and some others that use nominal classifications (not to be confused with check list schedules, useful as rough guides to further action only).

Why the Need for Precision?

The need for precision stems from the desirability to compare results from different samples taken at different times and places; to be able to evaluate mental development over a period of time; to judge the effectiveness of an intervention programme and make predictions with some degree of confidence.

Popular common knowledge is derived from a collection of specific and limited individual experiences, and, as such, is more in the nature of belief. It has a place, in that it offers some personal sense of security/competence in the day-to-day management of children and in personal self-management. However, it is neither reliable nor valid as it is not open to checks and functions on particularities of information, often due to chance factors. To satisfy the need for precision, a measurement demands a standard unit of measure and a standardised measuring instrument that is universally applicable and accepted as reliable, so that the resultant measurement can be trusted.

In the case of norm-based individual tests of mental development, we need to have a scale that allows comparisons of results over time in a variety of situations, both in the practical diagnostic settings and in the follow up of special groups. In the hands of the expertly trained, the scientific methodology used in the measurements derived from norm-based tests of mental development can achieve the high degree of precision required for research purposes and epidemiological studies.

In summary:

- In general, within the limitations of the tests, some degree of precision is needed in formulating an assessment of mental abilities.
- In the individual case, measured values have to be precise enough over time to be used to monitor the individual progress in development, or the effectiveness of a training programme. More importantly, however, the measured values should be meaningful and valid for the individual case.
- In research programmes, a high degree of reliability and precision is required of any measurement.

5 About Individual Tests of Mental Development

Introduction

The old tests of intelligence such as the Binet (1916)and the Wechsler Intelligence Scales for Children (WISC-R; Wechsler, 1976) covered a wide age range, from 3+ years to 16 years. The more modern tests of mental development, like their predecessors, are also norm based but cover shorter age ranges. This makes possible a wider coverage at every age level. Originally, tests were standardised on an American population, but very quickly UK standardisations appeared.

Nowadays, most tests of mental development are designed to tap the abilities of children from 1½–8 years. A couple of tests start from birth (within a couple of weeks or so). Nearly all come with clear instructions, helpful scoring guides and are attractive to young children. Some also offer training material for the users. They all mostly follow the conventional practice of setting the mean point value at 100 and a *SD* around 15 points so that results between tests become comparable (provided they are all based on a large sampling of population in their standardisation and not restricted to a specific type or group).

Standardised scores derived from a norm-based test prove to be most reliable for values around the mean. Scores at either extreme ends of the distribution range are less reliable. This is more noticeable in the case of young children, whose scores extend either above or below the range of the test used, as obviously the test has not fully tapped their abilities or deficits.

Test Content

All psychological tests of mental development for children use similar batteries of test materials, such as: small bricks to hold, build or count with; beads to thread; form boards to complete; pictures to identify or arrange in sequences; patterns to copy; balls to throw, catch, roll; rings to hold and dangle; bells to ring; pencil-and-paper tasks; sentences and digit sequences to repeat; objects to name; pictures to describe, arrange or use; problem situations to resolve.

In other words, all tests of mental development have specific sets of tasks that have to be presented in a systematic and standardised way to the child to elicit interactions necessary to reveal the underlying thinking structure displayed in the consequent behaviour/performance. Whether the test results are considered to be expressions of a general level of "intelligence" or "mental ability," or indicate levels specific to certain areas or channels of functions, the ultimate aim is to establish the efficiency or otherwise of the mental processing system of the child under examination. All tests of mental ability provide tables for translating raw scores into mental age (MA), standard score (SS), IQ and percentile rank equivalents.

The main source of variation between the contents of tests is found in:

- The choice of the material used and in the size, shape, colour, design of the test objects. Most tests nowadays are colourful; objects used are familiar and designed to appeal to children.
- The verbal instructions for administering the delivery of the test items as well as in the way they are presented.
- The age range covered in the standardised sample.
- The areas of functions tested.
- The length of time required to administer the test.
- The amount of helpful instruction and guidance provided, in other words, the "user-friendliness."

For babies aged 0–2 years and very young children, 2–8 years, it is pertinent to mention the Griffith Mental Development Scales 0–2 years (GMDS, 1954, 1996 Huntley revision), the Griffith Extended Mental Development Scales (1970), and of 2–8 years (Faragher update GMDS-ER, in press), the Bayley Scales of Infant Development (2nd Edition) (BSID-II, 1993) and the Wechsler Pre-school and Primary Scale of Intelligence – 3rd UK Edition (WPPSI-III UK, 2004) as they all cover all or parts of this age range and have very recent UK standardisations.

. For the young child, WIPPSI-III UK 2.6 years–7.3 years divides into two age bands: 2.6–3.11 years and 4.0–7.3 years. This enables assessors to better describe individual performance relative to the appropriate reference group, with VQ, PQ and GQ measures and profiling within these functions. These tests provide six verbal scales for a verbal quotient (VQ) and six performance scales for a performance quotient (PQ). They offer a comprehensive sample of mental abilities in young children in the UK and allow a better understanding of the relative performance of clinical and non-clinical groups.

The GMDS-ER 2 years–8 years, like its predecessor GMDS, offers a similar profiling of specified areas of function in verbal, performance, gross and fine motor control skills, with the possibility of extending downwards to tap the abilities of the underachievers by using the protocol of the GMDS 0–2yrs. The GMDS-ER adheres to Griffith's claims to measure the development of "the various avenues of learning," but describes the test items used in terms of their underlying constructs.

At the infant age levels, the BSID-II, age range 1 month–42 months, and the GMDS, age range 0–2 years, are the two most used tests in the UK. The GMDS 0–2 years was the first test for use with infants from birth designed to cover mental abilities over five areas of development. Both these infant scales attend to aspects of motor as well as language aspects of mental development; they both tap the emergence of fine and gross motor skills as well as verbal and coordination skills, but the GMDS 0–2 years offers a more comprehensive profiling, something which is very helpful for diagnostic purpose.

The BSID-II offers results as a mental ability level MQ, a performance ability level PQ and a general level GQ also based on a variety of subtests and profiling of abilities, and includes motor functions useful for diagnostic purposes.

Individual tests of mental ability tend to be rather lengthy. The older the child the longer it takes. In practice, on average one should allow at least 30–45 minutes for young infants and as much as 1–1.4 hours for older children. Generally, in the past, these tests were not always user friendly but recent updates have remedied this to some extent. In addition some tests like the WIPPSI-III UK allow shorter versions to be administered by selecting items according to age levels, and a scoring sheet with quick access to standard scores. The BSID II has a similar option for applying selected items only. The GMDS and GMDS-ER offer no short cuts or selective testing, but continue to provide profiling across 6 areas of functions.

Nowadays, individual tests of mental ability also include more than administration and scoring guidance; they also provide facilitators. For example, WIPPSI III UK includes a behavioural observation sheet to guide recordings of the child's presentation, behaviour, mood, etc. The BSID II adds a similar behavioural observation sheet plus a parental evaluation questionnaire.

The GMDS-ER provides a technical manual with test construction details, a separate administration manual with descriptive constructs of test item details, clear administration procedures, and a comprehensive scoring sheet with colour guide.

In the immediate future, the GMDS 0–2years (Huntley revision, 1996) and the extension 2–8 years (GMDS-ER) (Faragher, in press) are likely to become even more appealing to their users because they are comprehensive and have been made more user friendly in design by including most of the facilitators mentioned above while continuing to offer profiling of results across six different areas of observation.

The general tendency is towards making individual tests of mental development more user friendly by providing additional material and information, such as described above, plus guides to report writing, comprehensive and easily accessed scoring sheets, automated scoring systems with a variety of facilities and training videos. Colour is also more frequently used on materials for easier recognition, coding and eye appeal.

More importantly perhaps, individual tests of mental development have a "use by date" to keep in step with the changing nature of both our modern life style and social/cultural/educational/health environments, which are likely to affect children's perceptions, their fields of interest and introduce variations in their range and rate of learning. Over a period of years, content and results derived from norm-based individual tests of mental development have to be revised and re-standardised to new norms to yield reliable and valid results.

A note of caution: The revised scoring sheet of the GMDS-ER 2–8 years incorporates the whole of the 0–2 (1996, Huntley revision) scoring sheet. As such the GMDS-ER scoring sheet may appear to provide a measure of mental development in a continuum over the age range of 0–8yrs. But this is not so. There are two gaps: a time gap of 8 years between the respective standardisations of the two tests and an age range gap between the GMDS 0–2 years and the GMDS-ER 2–8 years samples. This latter did not sample any children in the 0–2 years range, only in the 2+ years range. The 0–2 yrs GMDS remains specifically a test for the assessment of mental abilities for babies and young infants of CA 0 months–23.9

...s, and the GMDS-ER (in press) specifically for young children of A 2 years1 month–7+ years.

The case of severely underachieving children who score at the lower limits of any norm-based test of mental ability is a special one as their achieved standard score (SS) is not very helpful. For the individual child in this tail end position, it is more meaningful to consider the descriptive nature of the items contributing to the SS results rather than their numerical value. In other words, an analysis of the test items achieved and/or failed with their MA equivalent would provide information more likely to be of practical value in designing any intervention programme for accelerating, correcting or facilitating developmental ability. Such descriptive evaluation would also be more meaningful and helpful to the parents.

In addition, it is essential to remember that all psychological tests of mental development are designed to tap observable mental functions in the individual case, in other words, they tap the outward displays of mental ability. While the results derived from norm-based mental testing may point to some sensory deficits and neurological or physical problems, they do so only in relation to other individuals of the same age group sampled from a "normal" population; that is, a population that does not include individuals with known sensory deficits and/or neurological/physical impairment. Furthermore, while such tests tap the full range of mental function they do not take into account the condition of a premature birth.

Generally, mental development tests are designed to structure the scoring to enable the skilled user to make sense of the results as diagnostic pointers as to how the mental ability of an individual varies in performance in relation to the various areas of function observed at the time. As such, therefore, tests of mental development in the individual case can be said to be potential diagnostic tools helpful to facilitate intervention programmes to repair, improve or restore the efficiency of the function of the mental system. Professional practitioners other than psychologists using such tests may derive clues, through their observations of the child's interactive behaviour, more pertinent to their specialised fields in child development. Useful as this may be, it does not form part of the diagnostic potential of the test scores. Results derived from a test score and results derived from observations during the interview situation should not be confused.

All norm-based individual tests of mental development are lengthy. The precision, reliability and validity of their results rest on whether they are appropriately used and skilfully applied. They should not be used a routine procedure. Check lists are criteria-based schedules. They look discrete stages of developing abilities and are quick and easy to administer. They are suitable for routine use as pre selectors for a more precise and comprehensive assessment.

Structure

Tests vary in the way they are structured. Usually a dichotomous distinction is made between activities requiring verbal responses and those requiring practical activities.

The WPPSI tests use this classification to structure the application of the items into two sections, with all the verbal type items in one and all performance (non-verbal) type items in the other. This allows for computing separate equivalent standard scores. These are named accordingly as VQ (verbal quotient) and PQ (performance quotient).

The BSID II uses a "mental" and "motor" terminology for its dichotomy, with resultant mental quotients and motor quotients as standard values.

Tests like the old Binet and the Terman Merril select test items according to age year rather than areas of function. Thus, verbal and performance tasks are mixed within each age year. These tests yield a general standard score, the GQ, which stands for general intelligence. Such tests do not allow for any comparison within the results between verbal and performance abilities. It was held at the time that there was only one general factor of mental ability: the factor "g" for intelligence.

Nowadays the concept of a general intelligence, though not invalid, is not considered useful in identifying areas of weaknesses and/or strengths in the display of mental abilities in the individual case. As already mentioned, tests, such as WIPPSI III UK, measure at least the verbal/performance dichotomies, while others, such as the GMDS and GMDS-ER and the BSID II, assess various areas of skills. This allows for separate developmental quotients (SQ) according to the number of areas tested, which can be displayed as individual profiles with immediate diagnostic appeal. They also offer a general quotient (GQ), which is derived from the sum total of scores obtained from the subscales.

Packaging

All developmental tests require a variety of objects and other material as test items. These are generally delivered in hard or soft containers, the size of a small portable case that is not too heavy to carry about. Perhaps a case on wheels may be the choice design in the future. There is room for facilitating the selection of test items/material required during an interview session as well as a need to ease the problem of weight.

The latest BSID II container is bulky, heavy and most difficult to carry about. It may have been so designed on purpose, intended to be a piece of installed equipment in the assessment room. There is a possible advantage to this as the test material is more easily kept safe from damage or loss. However, as this test offers the option of using test items selectively, the size and weight of the box may not present as a great handicap. BSID III (2005) has just introduced a case on wheels.

Generally users prefer a piece of portable packaged test equipment designed to be easily carried about to various centres, convenient for parents with young children or for the occasional home visits. Hopefully, new revised tests may soon appear packaged in a practical sized case on a removable wheel system.

Users are urged to lobby test publishers so that test publishers are more aware of practitioners' needs with respect to packaging and other issues as well.

Section Three: Issues in Application

In this section we focus on the practitioner skills necessary for effective assessment of the young child.

6 Common Errors During the Assessment Interview

Introduction

Whatever their contents, structure and packaging, all tests require the same high degree of adherence to their prescribed procedures for administration and of consistency in the scoring of their results. The provision of guides to users and facilitators may be helpful additions, but none guarantees the elimination of error in their usage simply because errors occur in a multitude of ways.

It is also important to remember that all measurements are liable to errors. When these involve infants and young children, errors are unavoidable as their skills are not established and their attempts to display them are often of an experimental nature. Infants and young children are likely to be unreliable. It is worth pointing out that while the assessor is searching for evidence of developing mental skills, the child is mentally challenged to demonstrate his or her skills. It is also important to remember that both the searching for and the demonstration of ability rest at a point in time and represent only a static sampling of a dynamic ongoing process.

In the individual testing situation, both assessor and child are in a learning situation and liable to trial-and-error strategies. Common errors, which could endanger the reliability of the scores and invalidate the sampling of the child's mental ability at the time, apply to all tests and arise in a variety of forms, some of which include variables apparently not accounted for in the construction of the tests, such as, for instance, the time of day testing is carried out or the environmental situation.

In the UK nowadays, many professionals involved in the applied fields of medicine, psychology, education and social services have seen their work space shrink with shared usage and cluttered up with a growing amount of equipment, while their work time has lengthened and they have increasingly been burdened with an overloading of duties. They have adapted and come to accept their situation, even to perceive it as normal. To external observers such as parents, however, they present like a fast forward video imaging in cramped conditions and as such not conducive to putting their clients at ease and more likely to produce errors.

From start to finish, the testing situation is liable to trap the inexperienced user into making errors. These occur in various ways, and for different reasons. They occur in different areas of the assessment procedure. For the sake of clarity, some common errors have been described below, classified according to where in the testing procedure they may occur.

The Assessment Setting

The ambience of the room in which the assessment takes place induces an affective state in the child. What may appear a normal setting to adults can be unsettling to a young child. An overcrowding of strange towering adults around the child overwhelms, makes for apprehension, may arouse suspicion in the young child's mind and creates feelings of insecurity. As a result, a young child may: cling to his/her parent, regress by accepting only very simple tasks, or may become tentative in responding to the point of even refusing to participate altogether.

A setting full of toys within easy reach and colourful posters on the walls (perhaps because the waiting room was the only empty space available at the time) makes for distractions and frustrations, as the child would naturally like to explore and experiment. Such a distracting setting reduces the efficiency of the child and endangers the reliability of the results. It could also lengthen the whole proceedings of testing, sometimes well beyond the threshold of the child's endurance. To set a testing interview in a screened off section of a school dining hall, or in a corner of a seminar room or in a play room, does not provide an appropriate venue either.

Seating requires attention as regards issues of adequate support and adjustable height levels for the young child in assessment, and of appropriate positioning of the accompanying parent(s). When seated at a table to carry out a task the young child needs to be well supported and comfortable, in a state of stable equilibrium with freedom of hand, arm and shoulder movements to allow for good control in reaching and manipulating objects unhampered. In the situation where an infant is held on a mother's lap, again adequate seating for the mother should place the baby close to and at an appropriate level with the table surface to allow the baby to reach and handle test items. In other words, to enable the infant to demonstrate how his developing motor functions are put to use. Poor performance could result from awkward positioning rather than reflect poor mental function or physical immaturity.

Particularly in the older age range, a child who is freely mobile and physically active should not have to kneel on a low chair in order to carry out tasks, nor be placed too high over the table surface (whether standing or seated). Bodily discomfort is liable to induce wriggling, shifting position, even climbing onto the table, thereby diminishing the child's focus of attention on the task and distracting the observer.

Young children tend to want their parent close by, and parents are curious and want to be able to watch their child's performance; some of them may be somewhat apprehensive, especially if it is their first experience of psychological investigation.

Placing the parent in full view in front of the child is not a good idea especially if the parent is anxious or tense. Young children are sensitive to facial expressions, especially those of their parents. Experience shows that placing a parent side by side with the child encourages a parent-child interaction, may prompt the parent to help the child, and tempts the child to turn to the parent for help. It is not uncommon to see a young child actually taking hold of the parent's hand in an attempt to get the parent to perform the task, or be shown how it is done.

Some tests, such as the WIIPSI III, give specific instruction on positioning and require the child to be seen alone during the testing situation, while others give no guidance on this point.

The Social Skills of Engagement

It is natural and necessary for an infant to interact with its environment in order to acquire information leading to knowledge. There are different forms of interaction, but when a self determined activity is pursued from choice (or in the case of infants pursued in a haphazard way) and for its own sake and enjoyment, it is called play.

In our modern culture, this form of free play activity has come to be almost entirely associated with and restricted to childhood. It is considered pleasurable for those involved in play and hence viewed as a desirable activity to pursue with children. It is not surprising, therefore, to find that inevitably when adults are involved with young children they attempt to create a play-like situation (see J. Piaget's developmental stages and R. Griffiths on play in the references and Appendix 5)

When in a testing situation with children, however, there is also the need to satisfy the aim of the test in order to achieve reliable psychometric results of the child's mental ability from the interactive process set up at the time.

There is a delicate balance between a relaxed friendly but controlled approach that respects the standardised procedures and the individuality of the child within the testing situation and the setting up of a play session with choices of alternatives that gives the child some control. The first facilitates observations of response to testing, the other runs the risk of endangering the delivery of the standard procedures, of creating muddle in the observation of the responses, and would tend to prolong testing time. Such errors can be said to derive from inadequate engagement with the child in the testing situation and may reflect the following:

a) The Assessor's Need to Please

Quite often, whether through a desire to please or a lack of confidence, the assessor adopts an overly solicitous approach. Parent and child are offered a variety of options. For example, asking, "Where would you like to sit," or by giving the child an option of refusal by asking, "Do you want to do this?" or "Do you want to play with this?" By framing the requests in this way, the assessor is sending the false message to both parent and child that there is a free option, which in fact does not exist, since the purpose of testing is to elicit responses to set tasks through rigid standardised procedures.

This sort of engagement is as fraught with difficulties as is an over enthusiastic and precipitous plunge, which overwhelms the child with a verbal overflow of superlatives "My what a lovely dress, doesn't your mummy dress you prettily" or "What a big boy – I bet you are very, very good at doing lots and lots of things," "Come and look ! I have heaps of toys and things for you to play with."

It is far better to try and establish a mutuality of interest. When the young child is old enough (2+ years) it is possible to do this with basic language and coordination skills. One way to establish a mutuality of interest is by starting the process of introductions with an exchange of first names. Begin by offering "My name is ..."; or "I am .... ," then by asking the child "What is your name?" and/or "Who are you?" Next explain the purpose of the interview by saying something like: "I have different puzzles and fun tasks here," and invite the child with a gentle "Come, let's see now what we can do."

During the course of the interview, the assessor may be tempted to use praise in order to encourage the child to achieve as much as possible. Free and indiscriminate use of praises may prove counterproductive, as, for example, in the use of "Bravo, – that's very, very good, – well done" especially if applied on every occasion and almost automatically. It is better to express an appropriate approval by saying, "That's good, I think you have enjoyed this task" or quietly say, "Well done, that was a good try" after a serious attempt on the part of the child to complete a difficult task.

b) Missed Opportunities

Often children volunteer information of a personal nature such as "My brother has ... or does ...", or makes a spontaneous comment such as "Dogs like to play ..." Such unsolicited information offers the assessor an opening gambit, an opportunity to engage the child in conversation, which should never be missed. The child can be easily coaxed by responding and showing interest with simple follow up questions like "Really, tell me more" ... or "Do you have a dog? What's your dog's name?" This allows the assessor to sample more of the child's ability in the use of speech and language.

Parental Preparation

For a psychological investigation to proceed smoothly, the parent needs to be well informed as to the purpose of the test, its advantages and its limitations and the procedures involved. Inadequate information about the test given to a parent prior to assessment may lead to misunderstandings and may raise false expectations either of which can affect the attitude of the child during the interview.

There are fairly frequent examples where the parent imagines the interview to be just a form of play session and has told the child just that; or where an over anxious parent has understood the test to be a kind of exam, and has stressed to the child the importance of "passing" the test in order not to let down the parent. Such undesirable situations, which lead to problems during and/or after assessment, can be avoided by spending more time with the parent prior to the interview to clarify points of issues and answer any query raised by the parent.

Test Administration

Because of the nature of their work, most professionals may have to keep the demands of a diversity of tasks not fully resolved in their mind during their working day, which may induce a state of preoccupation and prove distracting. Testing children is a lengthy procedure requiring not only just a long period of time but a long period of sustained attention.

When engaged in testing, the scoring sheet is used to allow for entries of credits to be made as the testing proceeds. Most psychological test items are only presented once, but they can be credited at more than one age level according to the speed of successful completion or complexity level achieved in multi level tasks. Consequently, the scoring sheet often enters the same test items at different age levels. Users, when engaged in the testing situation, should credit a test item according to its success level, but if the item has been passed successfully at its highest level then all the lower levels indicated on the scoring sheet for the item should be automatically credited.

Some trainees (or inexperienced users) tend to use the scoring sheet as a guide to present the test items, and follow the entries on the scoring sheet, forgetting or ignoring the instruction given in the manual regarding the correct presentation of test items. However, unless one is very familiar with and proficient in the use of a test, relying exclusively on using the scoring sheet as a guide to present items increases the risk of repeated presentations, sometimes modified to fit with the grades of difficulty shown on the scoring sheet. This would introduce a practice effect and lengthen testing time. There is also an added risk of varying the verbal instructions. The net result is the possibility of muddling the child and invalidating the results.

The following examples are given as illustrations from:

1) The GMDS Threading Beads to Coloured Pattern [in the Hand Eye Coordination Subscale, Year 3]

The verbal instructions for this item: The assessor points to the lace with the completed pattern (of 12 beads:3 green, 3 red, 3 yellow, and 3 blue beads), drawing attention to the arrangement and says: "Look at my pretty necklace with lots of colours in a pattern" then point to the box with coloured beads and another lace with 1 green bead already tied on to it, demonstrating to the child by threading 2 green beads. Then the assessor removes these 2 green beads and pointing at the completed sample left on the table asks: "Make a necklace just like this one." This test item can be presented to a 3–5 year old. It can be credited at:

i) 3 year level, which accepts just the threading of 6 beads but not to the pattern;
ii) 4 years, which requires 11 or more beads to be threaded but not necessarily to the pattern;
iii) 5 year level, if the 12 beads are threaded according to colour pattern correctly.

This test item is administered only once and scored according to the level of achievement.

The user who overlooks the restrictions of the standardised procedure, but is guided by the scoring sheet, which shows credit level entries at the 3, 4 and 5 year levels, may present the item according to the age of the child, varying the verbal instructions to fit in with the criterion demanded at each level in turn. As mentioned already, such multiple presentations lengthens testing time, introduces an element of practice, which invalidates the scoring and may create confusion, or bore the child.

2) BSID II. The Discrimination of Size Test subtest items: (163a, bowls and orange; 163b, boxes and lid; and163c, cubes)

These items form a sequence of pictures of similar objects in three different sizes on a card. Each sequence is associated with the picture of a single object presented on another card. There are three different sets and each set has to be given. In the first set, 163a, the child is presented with the picture of a large orange and a card with the pictures of three bowls similar in shape and colour but of different sizes.

The verbal presentation asks:

> Which bowl is the right size for my orange. Which bowl is not too big and not too small." The administrative instruction is : "If the child succeeds, proceed to the next series, and if the child fails, proceed with a demonstration of the item and give no further help, then carry on with the further sets as entered in the guide book to the end of this test.

Here again a poor administration can easily occur if the helpful demonstration is not followed correctly but given only at the end of the whole series of sets for the child to try again, or if helpful demonstration is given after each sequence. Invalidation in the scoring would occur in either case.

3) The WIPPSI III UK, the BSID II, the GMDS and GMDS-ER.

Again, the tasks of pattern making, whether with flat two dimensional material or with three dimensional cubes, get credited at different age levels. Similar lapses of memory or confusion between scoring sheet entries and administration guide instructions could lead to errors in sequencing or multiple presentation, which could invalidate the scoring for this item.

In order to achieve consistency of delivery, two conditions have to be met from the start: First, both the administration procedures as per test requirements and the verbal instructions for each test item should be applied precisely and verbatim. Second, the way to correctly present each test item has to become an established habit.

If for any reason failing memory raises some doubt as to the correct procedure, it is vital to go back to the test manual, rather than guess, so as to reinforce correct learning and establish consistency of delivery. To simply carry on improvising either or both aspects of the administrative delivery is almost fatal as it prevents habit formation and could induce chronic inconsistency of delivery.

Demonstration of a task is achieved through an ordered sequence of performance with test items. It must be slow, deliberate and clear. Presenting only part of the sequence for a task or rushing through the sequence too quickly can be mystifying to the child, as would be demonstrating a task to the child when the child has been distracted and is not watching.

The following illustrates how not to present a demonstration: in the colour pattern copying tasks, quickly assembling the bricks for the demonstration pattern in the palm of one's hand (as has been known to happen) out of sight of the child's view, then presenting it completed on the table with a request for the child to make one like it, amounts to performing "magic." It may bewilder the child rather than instruct him or her. Such errors would invalidate the resultant performance.

In addition to a sloppy attitude towards the rigors of following standardised procedures, a disregard of scoring instructions and the lack of professional objectivity, there is the problem of the "helping hand" It is sometimes difficult to resist helping a struggling child. This may amount to teaching. Errors are introduced when helping a struggling child to complete a task and then repeating the task, or by simply repeating a task in fragmented presentation or by giving the child a second chance when none is permitted. Any extra exposure to the test item has a teaching effect, which may result in boosting the score or boring the child.

As humans we are unpredictable and this makes it difficult to ensure an error free presentation of test items even in the experienced user. The case of the paediatrician who persisted in poorly administering the simple and common test item of "making a brick walk" is given as illustration.

The instruction and demonstration for this test item is clear and simple: "Let's make a brick walk. I'll show you." The brick is held between the thumb and two fingers and made to progress forward along the table surface by a series of short low hops. The child is then told: "Now you make the brick walk, make it walk like I did."

This particular paediatrician, although corrected in training, persisted in making the cube advance on the table by rolling it along held between thumb and two fingers: a somewhat awkward manoeuvre. She considered her way more representative of walking.

This anecdote illustrates both the strength of an individual belief and a lack of psychometric appreciation. A user may think or prefer a different way of presenting a test item in the belief that it is a better way. Indeed, sometimes there may be better ways of wording a presentation or of demonstrating a task. But such thinking is irrelevant, because the way a test item is presented has been standardised: applied in the same way in all cases in the sampled group. It is a standardised procedure used in the construction of the test. Consequently, any deviation from the standard procedure may change the very nature of the task and thus invalidate the test result.

Confusion is another source of error. This is less common, but may occur in the case where the professional assessor has to apply the updated test of a well used old version or where more than one type of similar tests are used during the working day. Under such circumstance a state of confusion in the way the test item is administered can easily arise, especially as some test items are very similar in type and appear in a number of different tests but require different presentation and scoring.

Scoring

Every test of mental ability has specific rules regarding the method of establishing a correct score and these should be strictly adhered to:

a) Base Lines and Cut-Off Points

As an illustration, when using the GMDS, failure to establish correctly a base line and a cut-off point can occur because the concept of 6 consecutive successes to establish the base line and 6 consecutive failures to establish the ceiling cut off point is not understood or is ignored. When this happens it automatically falsifies the results. Similar possibilities for making an error arise in the BSID II, where the three consecutive rule is frequently required to establish a cut off point in various areas of the test schedule. In the Binet Test, all the items in an age range have to be successfully passed to establish the baseline age range, and all items have to be failed to establish the ceiling cut-off age point. In some other tests (such as WIPPSI/Terman Merrill) failure to give correct weighting to scores also makes for erroneous scoring values.

b) Working out a CA (Chronological Age)

Whether chronological age is calculated in terms of years, months and weeks or years and months according to the requirements of the test, it may seem surprising (but not infrequently noted) that manual calculation of the chronological age of the child at the time of the test proves to be a frequent source of error. This seems to be more frequent in the UK where the common practice is to enter a date with the day, month, and year in a left to right sequential order.

To calculate the CA of a child at day of test requires a simple subtraction: the date of birth of the child is subtracted from the date of test. This operation requires a left to right work sequence of years, months and days, and the CA itself is expressed in weeks or months and weeks for infants and in years and months for a young child.

This conventional ordering of dates (more specific to the UK) creates confusion and is a potential source for errors. Errors in the calculation of the CA invalidate the related MA and IQ scores. In some tests of mental development, such as the GMDS 0–2 years, a test age is also required. The test age rounds up the CA to the next month even if the excess is only of one day beyond the date of birth. For example,1) a CA of 9 months and one week becomes a test age of 10 months and 2) a CA of 24 months and 1 day becomes a test age of 25 months and is outside the age range of the GMDS 0–2 years. The test age is only used for the calculations of standard scores.

Users (especially in the UK) are reminded that age is easier to calculate if the order of entry of dates is set in reverse: as years, months, and days, which makes for consistency between recording a date and expressing an age. It is worthwhile adopting this simple solution and an example of it is given in Table 2 below. An easy way to calculate age

Table 3. Calculating age

	Year	**Month**	**Day**
Date of test	2003	11	25
Date of birth of child	2002	5	6
Age of child	1	6	19
CA	18 months 19 days. (GMDS 0–2: Test age: 19 months]		

Note. Nearly all tests have scoring CDs, which automatically calculate the correct age, provided all dates are correctly entered in the first place. This applies for any numerical entry, such as entering and summing up raw scores.

c) Faulty Recording of Observations

In whatever way this occurs, it may affect the allocation of credits. This applies particularly when allocating credits from memory rather than from a written record or by inadvertently placing a credit tick against the wrong test item. It is always best to check scoring entries and their numerical totals.

Scoring from memory is more likely to happen with the crediting of expressed speech, where evidence of levels of language development is made from memory of the language heard rather than from a written record of what the child actually said at the time.

Psychological studies have revealed that in our recall process we tend to complete unfinished visual patterns and faulty or incomplete language structures. For instance, an incomplete circle is seen as a perfectly completed one.

One study asked teachers to note the language used by the children in the classroom. Unknown to the teachers the classroom session was recorded. The study revealed that teachers, when reporting back what the children had said, unwittingly restructured the children's expressed phrases and ungrammatical sentences into correctly structured ones as would be normally heard in correct adult speech form.

d) The Human Element Again

Errors may also arise when credits are given from judgement, coloured by bias. Here are some examples;

- finding excuses for failure: "He could do it really but he is tired," or "I think he just does not like bricks" to explain away a failure
- dismissing a failure on a task from an assumed competence of the child by saying something like: "Well, he looks so bright, it is too easy for him, he is bored, mother says he can do it at home"
- assuming incompetence in the child: "He could not possibly do this"

Apart from a preset personal expectancy, there is also the danger of too much empathy with the parent's expectations in evaluating the child's achievements. To minimise error in this area, some tests have introduced guide sheets and questionnaires, thus, for example:

The BSID II has a comprehensive questionnaire that seeks to incorporate the parental views of the child's performance on the test to guide the final evaluation. It is somewhat labour intensive but useful in that it provides some consistency in the way parental views are gathered.

The WIPPSI III has a "Behavioural Observation" sheet which is helpful in directing observation of the child in 7 areas: attitude towards testing, attention, visual/auditory/motor problems, language, physical appearance, affect, unusual behaviour. The sheet offers blank spaces for the user comments. Naturally, it lengthens the testing situation

The forthcoming 2–8 years GMDS-(ER) may have a short evaluation form to guide the reporting of the test findings, which should facilitate scoring and evaluation. Such a guide to reporting could be helpful to the inexperienced in that it defines attitudes, moods, behaviour, etc, which can then be selected according to observations noted by the assessor during the testing interview. It should not lengthen interviewing procedure since it can be consulted/completed at the end of the interview.

The Care of Test Materials

Pressure of time and the need for expediency can lead to neglect in the care of the test material in a variety of ways.

a) Checking

There is the common habit of failing to check the contents of the test case as well as not sorting items back into their right order of presentation after a testing assessment has been completed. One way to avoid this problem is to develop the habit of tidying up after a session. It is quite in order (depending on the age of the child) when testing has been completed to invite the child to help collect all the objects and tidy up. By the way, the ability to help tidy up toys is part of the assessment of mental development in early childhood found in some test protocols and can be assigned a credit point.

It is also helpful to have a set of spare items readily available to users. This is useful in emergencies only but does not exclude due care of the test equipment. Another solution is for each user to have a personal test case. This, however, may not be financially possible but it would help ensure good care of test equipment.

b) Using Equipment to Keep the Child Occupied

Inevitably, it happens that sometimes the situation gets out of hand and, in an attempt to restore order, pieces of standardised equipment get handed to a child to play with for a while. Sometimes toddlers are allowed to wander about with a test item in hand such as a ball, a mirror, even scissors. Not infrequently, toddlers have been left to freely help themselves from an open test case left on the floor while the assessor is talking to the parent or is busy adding up scores. Such uncontrolled access may cause accidents. It may also pre-familiarise the child with the test pieces, which is a deviation from standardised procedure and potentially introduces error into the interpretation.

Some Practical Suggestions for Maintaining the Flow of the Test Session

Below we present some practical suggestions for maintaining the flow of the testing procedure and the interest of the child while still remaining loyal to the constraints of administering a standardised test.

1) Gathering essential information prior to administering a developmental test

At the very least, it is important to know the age of the child and the reasons for the investigation in order to be able to:

- Choose an age-appropriate test.
- Select some test objects most likely to appeal to the child and have these ready to hand to make a good start.
- Identify the possible areas of difficulties deduced from the reason given for referral and prepare strategies to avoid problems accordingly. For example if there is a reported speech problem, be prepared to use non verbal performance tasks first.
- Do not proceed to exhaustion on a verbal performance task if the child struggles and appears frustrated. Break off and introduce another task before returning to complete the verbal performance test items.
- Provide relief in between verbal tasks by offering non-verbal tasks

and vice versa . A similar strategy would be followed where, for example, difficulty with hand control is reported. In such a case verbal tasks may be best to start with.

2) When a child has poor attention

- The room setting should be visually peaceful: tidy and uncluttered.
- Ensure as far as possible the elimination of distracting features such as large toys and dazzling posters.
- Remain friendly but firm and decisive in manner. Show no hesitation in the presentation of instructions.
- Whatever the age of the child do not make an issue of any display of disruptive behaviour such as, for instance, wandering about the room, accessing the test material box, scattering test material off the table. With very young infants the parent may be drawn in to help. With the nursery and infant school aged child one can say "No, we don't do that here" and use gentle persuasions, arouse curiosity, create a diversion but remain firm to demonstrate that you are in control. With an older child, one can use language to express why a specific behaviour is not acceptable, in other words, reason out the situation This does not apply to children diagnosed with severe hyperactivity disorder (HD) or attention disorder (AD); they require more specific handling.

3) Know the scope of your test material

Whenever possible exhaust the "multiple use" test objects fully, it saves on time and holds the interest of the child. For example, small cubes/ bricks have a variety of usage; thus, according to the age range of the child, they can be used for constructing models from memory, counting, eliciting orally various concepts such as those of size and height.

4) Be sensitive to the affective state of the child

Boredom, frustration, disappointment can be spotted and dealt with. Usually a change of activity suffices. Avoid creating a negative mood in the child by persisting with tasks he cannot do. Let the child's performance guide your presentation. For example, if the child has shown a lack of interest in building bricks and has failed or refused tasks with bricks, shift to another type of test item and return to it later in the testing; all tests of mental development have a variety of items for both verbal and non-verbal tasks and for various levels of difficulty to make a flexible approach possible.

5) Be supportive

A timid or shy child needs a gentle supportive approach. Build up confidence in the child by starting off with simple tasks and continue now and then to give a simpler task at the end of sections/scales/parts of the test, especially if the child has found it hard work or appears to be upset by failures. Give the child "time space"; don't rush or hurry up a timid child. Do not appear critical of the presenting problem, be patient and carry on with the testing in a normal friendly manner.

7 The Task of Observation

Introduction

The measurement of mental ability is inferred through expressed behaviour, performance and language. For this reason, test-users must be competent observers. Observation like any other skill can be acquired through learning and practice. Although tests are basically observation schedules and as such direct the observation of the user, which simplifies the task of the user, there are pitfalls that need to be avoided.

Issues in Observation

a) Mistaking random activity for purposeful action

The testing of very young children is seldom easy and does not always proceed according to the book. Very young children do not appreciate the formalities of test administration. They lack the inhibition of social mores and tend to be self willed.

Let us consider a possible situation in the GMDS use of the cup, spoon, and saucer test, where the infant has to bring at least two of the three items into contact and meaningful interaction. The infant under observation may take up the spoon and put it to its mouth, then bang the spoon on the table and carry on banging randomly. During this random banging, the infant may accidentally hit the saucer and also at the same time spontaneously start banging the cup onto the table with the other hand. The infant has interacted with all the three items but not as if there was understanding as to their correct use, which is the criterion for a credit.

In the confusion of the activity generated by the infant, an inexperienced or distracted observer with a slight break in focus causing wandering attention may wrongly credit this behaviour with a plus score.

b) Difficulties co-ordinating tasks

A question often in the user's mind is how to remain well in focus during the testing situation and, at the same time, be expected to note with fidelity all observations when even a slight distraction may cause part of an observed sequence to be missed .The answer to this concern is that it can be done with practice. Having a thorough knowledge of the test and experience in its application plus a well prepared mental set for the occasion facilitates the ability to remain well focused.

c) Professional bias

Most physiotherapists, paediatricians or neuroscientists observing a young child busy on a task of construction with small bricks may, because they have been trained this way, automatically focus their attention more on the way the engaged hands, fingers and arms of the child move during the task as they would thereby derive diagnostic clues related to their professional knowledge. In such a situation, the delivery of the task itself may become of secondary interest and is not as carefully observed, or more likely may affect the scoring of the item.

Professionals trained in the use of psychological tests of mental development observing the same situation would tend to direct the focus of their attention onto the strategies used by the child in attempting to complete the task. In the case where a child presents with motor or sensory dysfunction, the trained professionals would choose a suitable type of test, one more likely to enable the child to tackle given tasks and demonstrate his or her mental ability levels.

d) Preconceptions

Personal experiences of children in one's entourage tend to establish preconceived ideas and expectations as to levels of performance generally expected. These tend to create a bias that affects the fidelity of reporting. In some cases, a bias or pre-conception may lead the assessor to omit or credit a test item without verification. Often this is done on the basis that "I know this child, it's too easy; mother says her child is too old for this kind of toy," forgetting that the toy is used in a specific way to elicit a specific response; or by crediting a failure as a pass judging "he's just bored," or "he does not want to do it, but I'm sure he can."

How to Improve Observation Skills

Observation of human performance, behaviour and language is a basic method of gathering the information necessary to understand and evaluate the psychological dimensions of the thought process. At the start, one has to decide what to observe, what to look for. Mental preparation is necessary to focus the directed attention precisely. Observation is a skill to be developed and can be improved by learning and practicing the strategies on how to look (see Holt & Reynell, 1970).

The natural tendency for an observer is to want to see as much as possible as quickly as possible. Observation of the general picture gives an overview impression. Observation of details alone takes the subject out of context. There is a need to attend to both the general situation and the specific details in order to improve the fidelity of report. There is a need, therefore, to learn to look at the general picture and the particular detail by repeatedly moving from one to the other.

Developing a sequence of observation to cover all the details required or adopting a systematic way of looking improves the accuracy of observation. Basically, psychological tests and check lists can be seen as protocols for observation and, as such, facilitate the task of observation. All individual tests of mental ability are designed sequences to guide the observation of the users. But this is not enough.

The observer has to learn to be consistent in recording observations. Whether the observation is a numerical count of a specific performance/behaviour or a written entry in descriptive terms, the need for consistency of recording remains the same. Using a standardised psychological test helps to achieve objectivity but does not guarantee consistency. Inconsistency of observation or recording makes for unreliability.

That the observer is not a blank sheet is a statement of fact we need to recognise and accept. The observer brings personal experience, interests, beliefs, bias and knowledge in greater or smaller degrees. The observer sees from the standpoint of an individually felt experience, and each observer will have a specific and unique standpoint. Being aware of this makes impartiality easier. To prejudge a situation or interpret a response distorts the observation.

In order to better keep an open mind, it is necessary for users to develop the habit of discussing their observations with other colleagues as much as possible. Discussion is the way the personal felt experience of a thought is revealed, compared and exchanged. Discussion between users is a good way to learn to appreciate the existence of other views, for there are as many ways to view an observation as there are observers. To be aware of this stabilises both the observation and its evaluation.

8 How Skilled Observation Assists Evaluation

Introduction

It is all very well to become a skilled observer but to make sense of observations, other than as a numerical score, requires taking into account the many aspects of the mental process underlying the observation. To do so one has to attend to various areas of expression. Here we consider observation of the areas of language, vision and touch.

The Area of Language (see Appendix 6 notes on language development)

Language is perhaps one of the most important human abilities because it is the expressive modality of thought which reveals the acquisition of categories, the formation of concepts, of establishing analogies and the development of the deductive process of the higher mental functions.

It has now been established that, even before birth, the human embryo in its fifth month responds to the spoken voice and shows a preference for its mother's spoken voice.

From the moment of birth on, the human infant enters into a dialogue with his or her world (i.e., his or her mother at first, then his or her environment), and proceeds through listening, sorting, selecting, ordering and structuring sounds to establish an understanding of language. Later, with physical maturity, comes voiced articulated speech.

The role of the mother-infant baby talk interaction, or "motherese," is crucial to this learning process. Motherese captures the attention of the baby and then motivates exchanges and through melodic intonations conveys affective values.

Careful observations show that the human infant, with all the limitations of an immature neuro/central nervous system, deploys evidence of sensory discrimination and expressive emotive capacity coloured by individual styling from birth on. The human infant's ability to acquire language is genetically based.

Psychologists and psycho-linguists have examined the elements of the genetically based mental technology that underlies all language systems and as that divulged by the child. Their conclusions are thought provoking mainly because this natural technology – somewhat unconsciously operated – is human specific, and it is through speech/language that we structure our world.

The stages of language development have been profusely studied and reported, and most tests of mental development have a graded vocabulary and listings of levels of speech and language skills. It is sometimes difficult to observe during an assessment session the very early sounds such as the infant's "ah" "ooh" and singing tones, unless these universally noted early sounds occur spontaneously. The observer may need to "coo" and make simple vowel sounds in play with the infant in order to elicit imitation. Imitation has been noted as one of the basic strategies the infant uses to acquire speech. Irrespective of age, most learning of skills is done by imitation.

As speech develops, it becomes much easier to observe through such tasks as object naming and picture description. By then speech has acquired a specific cultural sound. Environmental influences affect the sound of speech and the structure of language and establish the particularities of different languages and the expressions of concepts specific to each one of them. (See Appendix 6 on language.)

The skilled observer would be sensitive to the underlying mental thought process revealed in language, which is more than speech. There is a receptive language and a passive comprehension, which is personal, and there is the mechanism of thought process revealed by the expressive language of speech.

Consider the following dialogue overhead between a father and his 2+ year old daughter in the preamble situation of a testing interview

"Daddy thez a back cat in the gad-den."
"Yes you're right. There is a black cat in the garden
But we say black. A black cat in the garden
What did you see in the garden?"

"A back cat in the gad-den, daddy," the voice explodes.
"No we say black, b-l-lack: black. A black cat
What did you see in the garden?"
With a steady gaze and a ghost of a grin,
The voice clear and firm dares a challenge
"A white cat daddy – a white cat in the gad-den."

Her punch line is delivered in the space of a few seconds. It is not part of a test item and cannot be credited but it provides information as to her mental process and will need to be acknowledged in the final statement of evaluation. This 2+ year old cannot as yet control her speech loop: vocal chords, mouth, tongue, lips, and neural pathways to deliver correct pronunciations. She has perceived the specific demand for the correct sound of a word, which she knows she cannot make. She substitutes a word she can correctly articulate: " white." Note, she uses another colour as colour is recognised as an identifying factor. She is not certain however that her solution is acceptable and offers it as a challenge. A conclusion derived from her facial expression ("the ghost of a grin, the steady gaze") and by the tone of voice ("clear and firm").

The spoken language in this example could be scored at different levels for her age: ability in articulation, ability to structure a sentence, problem solving skill.

The Area of Vision (see also Appendix 6 and 8)

Vision is an important sensory receptor as it enables the understanding of spatial appreciation, of direction, and the awareness of our position within space. Indeed visual experiences establish the structure of the space around us; they enable us to form an image of an outside reality and to project it back in its place.

Vision extends our space into distance, whereas other modalities (touch, smell and sound) are more limited. Touch, including tactile and kinaesthetic modalities, does not stretch beyond the immediate physical boundary of the body. Sound and smell modalities, while carrying over a greater distance, do not structure our space but merely fill it up.

Psychological studies of the blind from birth (Warren, 1984) have established the fact that blind people cannot structure space and thereby reinforce our common knowledge that recognises the need to provide guidance to the blind on the question of mobility and travel. On the other hand, more recent psychological research has also established that in the mental domain, even for those blind from birth, but otherwise physically and neurologically healthy, blind children show a mental development which follows in the normal way and they display higher mental processing abilities equal to those of the sighted (Hatwell, 2003; Warren, 1984).

Such findings suggest that the higher mental abilities of abstracting concepts and manipulating abstractions do not depend entirely on sensory input from receptors but derive from the perceptual system of the thinking process itself.

However, because vision is established from external concrete realities directly received and reinforced through other sensory modalities, such as those of touch, taste, smell and sound, visual experience is perceptually accepted as undeniable fact. The statement "I've seen it with my own eyes" is accepted evidence even in law. We still hold on to the practice of identifying a suspect by sight yet we all know that vision plays tricks with perception (Hatwell, 2003)

Despite the evidence of illusions and distortions (see Table 1 in Chapter 3), we continue to trust our visual reception; we still firmly believe in the evidence of vision. Sometimes it seems that to see is to know. We read facial expressions: a smile, a frown (see Appendix 8): We are fascinated by spectacles of magic (although we know they are products of illusion) and by the technically derived ultra sound and magnetic imaging.

Young pre-speech infants point at objects beyond their reach, smile at their mirror image and follow objects in flight; through their visual perceptions they learn to make sense of the world. Tests of mental development use all the sensory channels but the visual channel in particular is one of the main avenues for the acquisition and expression of learning. In the testing situation, both tester and tested rely on their visual input. The assessor observes and the child responds according to its perceptions. But individual perceptions and the structuring of individual learning are not necessarily the same: each assessor may gather different observations in the same way as each child may provide different responses.

Consider the following poem (Preston, 1993), which hints at the partial aspect of the reality as reflected in the application of ultra sound technology in common practice and which appears on the screen as by magic. Such an image is helpful and compelling to the professionally trained eye and viewed as true representation. A poet may perceive otherwise as follows:

Caught in the echoes of sound
The shape of a life to come
Patterns onto a screen
Scientific shadows of reality
Stamped with a seal of truth
Through the evidence of sight
This public blurred imagery
Brings instant knowledge
But held within the womb
In a bond of care
The foetus with its mother share
Felt experiences in privacy
The truth of their lives
Casts no shadows
Outlines no bounds
Tempers their soul"

The Area of Touch (see Appendix 7 on the hands)

Fingers, hands and skin are another important source of sensory input. Hands are the infant's early information channel for both self knowledge and knowledge of the outside world.

Through the fisted hand, then thumb and fingers, the infant learns about her-/himself as a taste and a feel of textures, later on in finger play s/he gets some information of movement, s/he explores her/his limbs, s/he finds the ability and the meaning of holding something and holding onto something, s/he discovers her/his physical structure, establishes her/his personal boundaries. S/he explores surfaces, feels textures and temperature variants, finds out about contours, holes and bumps, soft and hard, grasps, throws and controls. In short, the hand enables the infant to discover dimensions about her/his world which vision, sound, taste and smell do not convey. It is through touch that s/he comes to know. (Hatwell, Streri, & Gentaz, 2003).

It takes time for the hand (with its fingers, arm and shoulder support) to develop into a set of sensitive and precise tools, adaptable to a great variety of activities. It follows progressive stages and each one contributes to the mental development in the felt experiences they provide for the child.

The professional observer needs to know what to look for. Sketches of hand, finger and arm involvement in various tasks illustrate the salient aspects to look for in the observation of the early developing manual skills. (For further details and diagrams see Figure 7: with grasp, rotation, flexion and opposition of thumb, and pencil hold illustrations, and see Figure 8 for facial expressions.)

9 Facilitators and Promoters in the Developmental Process

Introduction

In this chapter, we are reminded of the individual nature of mental development, a process which is basically "self managed" and varies in style and scope according to the individual genetic structure and its environmental situation. Consequently, we need to view the parental/social nurturing aspects as having the potential to facilitate or obstruct the individual process of mental development.

The Child with Emergent Skills

The child participates in the process of learning from the very start. The observation of the child's activities, the choice and style of engagement used, suggest that they seem designed to empower the child with strategies to facilitate and promote mental development. Sometimes we identify these self monitored activities as play and sometimes we refer to them as practice learning. From the start, the infant appears driven to test out and practise his/her emergent skills, extend them and apply them to some purpose. Here we look at some of the various ways this happens.

Mobility

The ability to ambulate, to move one's body about, in however limited a way, establishes the awareness of boundaries: the boundaries of the body and the various and varied boundaries in existence in the world surrounding the body. It also brings about various degrees of independence. Being mobile provides opportunities to select an individual experience to unravel and make sense of. It appears that mobility promotes and facilitates learning from early infancy.

Mobility increases the infant's ability to direct his/her exploration and reach out into an extending world. The toddler does not remain a passive onlooker waiting for the external world to impinge on him/her. S/he sets about freely to discover the world, test out its limits. Moving about s/he gathers personal felt experiences as information to make sense of, to try out, and to store in memory.

The ability to move about accelerates mental growth by establishing and reinforcing the representations of neurological pathways and the growth of memory.

The particular style and manner of applying the last stages of newly acquired abilities are interesting to observe, for these reveal what the infant has found attractive in the environment; the strength or weakness of his/her curiosity to investigate and the style of his/her interactions and purpose.

The following excerpts from a descriptive poem entitled "Now Eve is One" (Preston, 1993) offers observations of early mobility and its extending effects on the acquisition of learning:

... Her most immediate needs simple
to explore what she encounters
to crawl about unhampered
but also to give chase
climb into the cat's basket
for a tight curl up and snuggle
an impelling treat
get to the top of the stairs
an irresistible challenge
... And now Eve walks pushing a trolley
crouches and straightens up
without toppling over
and chuckles as she grabs a hand
to go on her walkabouts
with flat feet and wobbly legs
she leaves footsteps behind ..."

Children test out their motor functions by running, jumping, swinging, balancing, etc. They repeatedly vary the parameters: longer, faster, higher. They establish graded stages to facilitate learning and delight in attaining the goals they set for themselves

Control of the Hand

Fine prehension accounts for the development of great manual precision and dexterity, which has enabled creative adaptation to tool a very wide range of tasks. From the simple use of a knife and fork, to the production of fine engravings, weavings, buildings or driving powered vehicles, the hand learns to perform complex and delicate tasks with great precision. Another brief excerpt from "Now Eve is One" (Preston, 1993) illustrates the role of the hand in the acquisition of learning thus:

To clutch a glossy magazine
watch the pages one by one
turn, crumple, tear into strips
a magic all absorbing"

Both humans and the higher apes have comparable hands and both make good use of their hands, which are adequately adapted to their needs. But humans have greater needs because of their more highly developed mental processing system. Their mental abilities outstrip that of the ape's and as a consequence humans have developed very precise and delicate fine movement control, which the higher apes do not possess (see Appendix 7 & 7a of the hand). Pre speech infants point to objects, animals and humans to indicate something they want, e.g., their bottle or the pack of rusks when they wish to eat or drink; on tests they can match shapes and sizes showing that they have acquired the concepts of shapes and sizes through the use of both their vision and their hands (and for those blind from birth through their hands alone), before having acquired the ability to use speech to name the concepts. Children's paintings and drawings reveal their perception of the world around them from their visual experiences; their drawing representation of the human figure reveals the progressive stage of their perceptual ability and manual skills. The "Drawing of a Man" test known as the Goodenough test (Goodenough, 1926) after the psychologist who designed it, is part of the battery of items of most mental development tests. From 3+ to 8 years, these drawings show a progressive perceptual representation from the simple crab like figure of "my mummy" to a fully clothed recognisable drawing of "my daddy."

Young children play with building blocks, colours, crayons and paints and household objects to create, copy, imitate over and over again. They use different materials and objects with similar strategies for exploration and practice. In this way, they consolidate and augment learning from a variety of repeated patterns of experiences derived from having to control the use of gross and fine hand movements.

Control of Speech (see Appendix 6)

Of all the human characteristics it is speech where the applied usage remains the most important. From the early cooing and singing sounds and babbled monologue through continuous practice and imitation of sounds, intonations, beats and rhythms, the acquisition of speech develops.

Together with the acquisition of speech there is also the formation of language to express thoughts and to communicate the individual felt experiences. Language, like motor skills, also liberates the child. Language skills continue to develop and to translate the contents of the mental thought process itself. Using language reinforces the development of the thought processing system. To do this, the child chants, rhymes words, chats, listens, questions, reports experiences verbally. The child reinforces his/her language skills constantly.

Consider excerpts from the poem "Lizzie in Words" (Preston, 1993), which describes a young child's strategy to develop her language skills. Rising 3 years of age she craves repetitions:

... ... I've arrived – I'm he-a!
My T-shirt displays images in colours
"Tell me the names" she asks
A tiger, a seal, a parrot and flowers
I enumerate pointing at each one
She nods. "Again" she demands
And I oblige expanding as I go along
Flower with leaves, a baby seal
A big tiger, a parrot with an orange beak
"Again" she asks and once more I repeat
Adding verbs to animate the scene
She confides "I don't like tigers the-a feess"

He is OK, he is a picture I reassure
"Tell me the names" she asks "make them talk"
Then quick with excitement she breaks off
Returns with soft toys and shares them out
With urgency demands as a treat
"We talk – we make them talk – now"
Story telling in a third dimension
As a world she fashions to her taste
Alive with all the words she's heard
To feel their meaning, know them
Take them as her own, become the words.
Like all of us, she's getting there
"I'm he-a! I've arrived!
Come with me"

Whether words lead to concepts or concepts lead to words, language contributes to the development of the mental processing of thoughts.

Language takes the individual out of isolation by permitting the development of thinking and the exchange of thoughts.

Language reveals that not every one perceives a piece of sensory received information in the same way, nor experiences mental activity in the same way. In order to dialogue successfully, individuals have to establish a common basis, a common understanding of the expressed thought or word in order to establish the mutuality of meaning required to advance a dialogue.

Memory

We have looked at the main modalities of the sensory system, which contribute most to mental development as a whole, and at the two main strategies (imitation and practice/repetition), which facilitate and promote mental development.

The efficiency of the memory system is crucial to learning. It affects the rate and breadth of mental development and the construction of an identity. The ability to store information and experiences and to retrieve them as required facilitates learning. Usually memory appears to be automatically carried out mainly because it normally operates almost instantaneously and without conscious effort.

Memory is not often thought of as a channel of independence because the independence it offers is of a mental nature characterised by its capacity of retention and speed of recall/recognition and of retrieval.

Memory enters into the equation of mental development and can be assigned a relative norm-based dimension. The acquisition of language is measured as the extent of vocabulary acquired, held in memory by the young child and is used as evidence of mental development.

Memory appears to be involved in all aspects of human activity and, depending on its degree of efficiency, it may accelerate or retard the speed of acquisition in learning. It is tested out with items such as the recall of sequences of digits and sentences graded in difficulty of size, the recall of shapes and patterns, of a musical score, etc., all of which are age related.

Memory tends to degrade with ageing. It is also associated with damage to certain areas of the brain suffered through injury or disease.

Sometimes memory is traced to some established neural pathways in the brain; sometimes it would seem to be held by a smell (the "Madeleine" cakes of Proust's childhood, 1982); or in the area of sound as a piece of melody; or in the area of vision as a colour; or movements such as observed in the dancer's choreographed limbs and the musician's trained hands after much sustained practice.

Sometimes memory appears to be retained through kinaesthetic experiences of an object, such as in the event reported by Jean Cocteau (1953) when, as a grown man, he first revisits the village of his childhood. He recounts how he retraces the steps of his daily path to school along a low stone wall expecting to recapture lost memories. Nothing happens until he bends down to the height of the young boy he had been. In this low position, he runs his hand along the stone wall as he used to do then. To his amazement and delight memories flood in. Did the stone wall store his memories?

Whether memory is held somewhere within the individual, and/or somewhere in some invisible mental field, it is usually helped into recall by prompts or associations with specifics of time, place, event, words, in the realities of the world. Its nature continues to baffle and fascinate. Imagine, what it might be like if you could not remember what you did, or heard, or saw from one moment to the next. Could you still have any sense of being somebody?

The Child as a Whole

As already mentioned we also use our limbs and our bodies to express something other than mere movement, something of the mental dimension involved in the control of movement: the purpose of the movement, such as, for example, dancers, marathon runners, or in the competitive displays of swimming, ice skating, gymnastics.

Consider the following poetical reporting (Preston, 1993) of observed gross motor performance in childhood:

Upside down on her climbing frame
Suspended at the knees
Look at me! Look at me!
At home the cry triumphant
Predictably raises a firm
Well done! Well done!
Heels anchored together
And like a spinning top
Multiple rotations on the spot
Beaming face. Gleaming eyes
The cry and response established ritual
Look at me! Look at me!
Well done! Well done!
First day at school she performs
Her acts of skilful dare.
Her peers are not impressed
They can swing precariously
Suspended by their feet
Dismay, disappointment diminish her.
The hurt spurs her on
Be as clever as the rest
Perhaps even better.
At home to face the challenge
Many keen practice sessions
Upside down on her climbing frame
She swings hanging by one foot
Look at me! Look at me!
The cry triumphant
Well done! Well done!
The echo reassures

Tomorrow she will show them!
Tomorrow her graduation time

In this descriptive poem, a rising 5-year-old child is learning to control her body and seems to enjoy extending her kinaesthetic feelings by repeated practice. She also displays the mental process in focussing her attention and in the strength of intention which directs and sustains her efforts at achieving the control of her body movements to her satisfaction. Note also the importance of the mother's presence and passive support.

This young child shows that she can marshal the control of her whole body to attain her desired goal: in this case to show that she is as capable as her peers or even better. Her display of physical prowess is like an act of love, a whole hearted commitment. It also reveals her ambitions, drives and social awareness: she can place herself in relation to her environment in order to break away from her private isolation. This desire to set oneself in a perspective, to participate within a group, stems from a mental process.

Her performance and the way she reaches her goal is a display of control of both her mental and physical skills. She orchestrates all her body skills and all her mental ability in partnership in her efforts to reach a goal she has set herself. It is a basic human operational process and each one has a particular style of displaying it. This operational process applies also to the child in a testing interview situation, and the skilled observer should note its individual particularities.

Many tasks in the testing situation provide opportunities to observe the operational process of the "whole child" in function. Take, for example, the task of completing form boards, a test item which appears in most individual tests of mental development. Some children approach the task in a haphazard trial-and-error way; some use spatial perception, selecting the right shape for the right space; some are hasty and appear careless in succeeding to fit shape to space neatly; others manipulate the shapes as if feeling them with their hands helps them to understand how to perform the task; some are slow and deliberate; some get frustrated when they encounter difficulties and give up at once; others persist in achieving correct placement. Form board tasks are timed and some children are eager to see if they can better their time when offered a second go, rushing the task carelessly; others do not lose their control of the task while concentrating on speed; others still are not particularly interested; and some choose not to have a second go. Two children may achieve the same score but their performance may vary greatly.

Form board tasks require spatial appreciation, manipulatory and hand-eye coordination skills, but the resolution of the tasks also require the application to focus on the tasks, to stay focussed until completion and to wish to do well. The individual characteristics of the mental elements involved in completing the tasks are observable as displays of style, application, determination, or lack of it, as well as the efficiency of motor control or otherwise. Altogether they reflect the way the child functions as a whole.

The Quality of Parenting

The term "parenting" refers to the task of parents (natural, de jury or de facto), teachers and all involved in the care of the infant/child through to adolescence or even beyond. Parenting is of great importance as it can facilitate and promote mental development.

In the early years, and with whatever resources available in the home and community, parenting operates in a one-to-one interactive situation and is dependent on the set of knowledge, beliefs, aims and motivations of the individual. Parenting is something like a catalyst, an agent that facilitates the transformation of two different elements to combine into a new and more complex substance. In a similar and somewhat mysterious way, parenting influences the child's acquisition of an identity and the making sense of the world s/he lives in.

Parenting is the quality of parental attention given to the needs of the growing child. Ideally, the task of the parent is to encourage, protect, stimulate, structure and create opportunities for the development of the child. Importantly, too, parenting imparts social and ethical values which shape behaviour. Good or efficient parenting that facilitates the provision of structures in the life of the child to enable the child to participate socially and enjoy the practice of skills, thereby also supports the child's endeavour to learn and to know how to behave. Sometimes, however, and for a variety of reasons, parenting does not act as a catalyst, it does not facilitate development but hampers it and it may even prevent the acquisition of learning in the child.

In testing children, the important role of the parent (and other parenting adults) does not cease to be operative even during the interview situation. It cannot be ignored. The assessor needs to understand the individual parenting of the child. The interview situation offers interactive possibilities for consultations with the parent, for eliciting parental views as to the resultant conclusion, and for getting to know the parental specific concerns as well as specific wishes, even before involving the parent in discussion over any envisaged decision making. It is important for the assessor and the parent to form a bond of trust so as to best resolve the needs of the child.

Whatever the user's degree of knowledge, training and experience, handling the resolution of any problem encountered during an interview situation according to prescribed suggestions does not exclude the use of commonsense.

10 Communicating Findings: How to Write a Report

Introduction

The testing of children's display of mental development, other than for research purposes, is not set up as a regular periodic check, as is done with screening procedures. The examination of the development of the mental process and its evaluation is a lengthy and complex undertaking and should be carried out only for a good reason, such as answering raised queries and doubts regarding the development of the child, or for the follow up of progress of intervention programmes.

Psychological tests of mental development are used to help identify and evaluate the underlying mental process displayed by a child presented with a problem, in order to help resolve this problem to the benefit of the child . If one is to achieve this aim, the foundation of the psychological testing tool cannot be ignored, nor its limitations. Having mastered test and testing, there remains the inescapable task of how best to communicate the findings.

The most common way is to write a report. On the basis that something thoroughly understood can be easily and clearly expressed, there should be no difficulty in writing an informative report. To write a helpful report, one has to have the required skills for organising the findings derived from testing and for translating them into a language meaningful to all recipients: the parent and the various professionals in the services concerned with child's health, education and social welfare.

Remember a report is not just about describing a test and summing up numerical results. The report is about describing a child as a whole, in a state of development in relation to a peer group. It is about finding out how a particular child is making sense of the world around her/him, how s/he is coping and where and how s/he is not coping with some aspects of the social, educational, or affective demands of her/his environment.

A written report is also a record for future reference. As such the report should not just inform as to the child's interactive abilities, it should contain relevant details of identification, levels of achievement, and recommendations. Organising the information under various headings helps structure the reported findings.

The Contents of the Report

Some individual tests of mental development include guidance on report writing. The following suggestions (not necessarily under the given order of the headings) represent a framework to structure all the necessary and essentials findings pertaining to the child as a whole.

Facts of Identification

- The name, gender and date of birth of the child
- The place and date of the investigation
- The age of infant/child at time of assessment
- The reason for the investigation.
- The referring agency
- The test(s) used in the assessment procedure
- The name of the assessor

Facts of Personal History

Any facts in the medical/social history or personal condition attending the child should only be given if relevant to the investigation and only with the knowledge and consent of the parent.

Observations Noted During the Interview

As a jog to memory for a later follow up, it is advisable to include observations such as, for example, brief comments on the presentation of the child at the time of testing, regarding physique, attitude or mood, degree of alertness, or co-operation. These are informative observations that may also be helpful to recipients of the report not acquainted with the child, and for comparison in follow up situations.

Updated tests include useful guides in this area. The new version of the WIPPI-RIII UK has a "Behavioural Observation" sheet for recording elements of observed behaviour, attitude and physique; the UK revision of the GMDS would also list aspects of behaviour to guide reporting and offers a "report" model. The BSDI II has a more extensive behaviour rating based on parental assessment of the child's performance and a rating scale covering various aspects of typical behaviour during testing.

Presentation of Findings

The main body of the report should contain the results of the assessment structured in ways to present both a general and a specific picture of the findings and which should describe pertinent passed or failed items to help the recipient appreciate what the numerical level of ability quoted represents in the realities of life.

The findings should be succinctly summarised to indicate the child's rank position within her/his peer group, as well as her/his own strengths and weaknesses. Depending on the test used, the range and diversity of the areas of function observed would vary.

Points to Remember when Reporting Findings

Whatever the professional field of investigative application, the diagnostic value of the findings must be meaningful and valid. Bear in mind that standardised scores that fall at the extreme ends of recorded distributions are somewhat meaningless, especially in children whose scores fall below the range of the test used. In such cases and in the absence of appropriate alternative tests, the qualitative description of observed ability/performance may prove more meaningful to the parent and other recipients of the report and more likely to help structure an intervention programme.

When reporting results obtained from a psychological test of mental development in infants, differences between IQ scores equal to or greater than 1 *SD* (=> 15 points) are probably not significant, but it is advisable to investigate differences of 2 *SD* (=>30 points) as these may be probably significant. In the case of infants in the 0–2 years of age range, great caution is advisable in assigning significance to score variations. The abilities of infants are variable and dispersed.

What is important to remember in quoting figures is to give them meaning as to what the figures stand for and what they represent. It is essential, therefore, to qualify the figures with descriptive equivalents and to provide some evidence-based information in support and clarification as to ability level with a few specific illustrative examples from the testing.

To illustrate, here are some examples from the GMDS 0–2 years:

Example A: Child CA, 10 months: The statement Motor Ability DQ 93–103 should be qualified immediately with a statement "of average level in motor development" for his age, and this in turn should be explained with factual information derived from the test results by quoting some of the achieved test items: " can pull self up by furniture, can stand holding on to furniture and side-steps round inside the cot," which are at average ability level for age.

Example B: Child CA, 8 months: The statement "does not hold three cubes yet" should be qualified by adding more positive observations of successfully achieved items: "but can rattle box, click bricks in imitation and lifts lid of a box," which are all age compatible abilities.

Final Evaluation

A summary is generally helpful to both the writer of the report and to the recipient. For the recipient, it clarifies the main issue(s). For the writer, it is a process of synthesis. It is the bringing together and the merging of all recorded facts with the evaluation derived from the personal experience of the testing situation in all its aspects. It is dependent on the degree of personal knowledge, experience and objectivity. Basically, it represents an objectively derived considered opinion.

The need for rounding off with a conclusion and recommended further action is obvious. A conclusion should be brief; present the salient points, clarify issues and hopefully resolve the initial query or suggest intervention plans to help satisfy the needs of the child, for the benefit of the child.

There is another consideration that applies only in the case of assessing infants and young children. It concerns the position and rights of the parent or guardian. In the UK these are covered by legislation.

Protocol and Parental Rights

- At all times the assessor has the interest of the child in mind. One could say that the assessor is accountable to the child. In this respect, both parent and assessor should have a common aim. There are exceptions and special cases that have to be resolved with thought and tact and sometimes in consultation with colleagues.
- Parents have the right to access the contents of any written report. It is desirable to be open and to draw parents into consultation throughout the interview.
- The parental wish for confidentiality has to be respected. It is important, therefore, to gain parental confidence throughout the investigation and secure their co-operation by consulting and discussing with them regarding both findings and needs.
- Any advice or referral to agencies and any action envisaged can only be made after consultation with the parent and with parental consent, hence the importance of Step 3 above.
- Any advice and recommendation involving other professional agencies should be realistic as to the possibilities of implementation so as not to disappoint or frustrate parents or create stressful situations. Knowledge of local amenities, in either the private or public sectors, is valuable and may help avoid difficulties.

Variations

The way a report is written and presented would vary according to individual style and specific professional requirements. Thus:

- Some may prefer to combine sections "jog to memory" and "final evaluation" immediately after the factual details of the first two sections. Then proceed to enter the results of test findings and then give their concluding resolution under a closing "further action section."
- Some may choose to report findings in descriptive terms and not quote figures.
- Some may prefer not to use standard scores but use percentile ranks instead.
- Some like to include a profile graph of results, others do not.

At all times, however, it is best to keep to the following principles:

- The practical details of identification, and relevant personal history to be entered first precisely and clearly for the recipient. For example, the age of the child at testing should not be left for the recipient to work out.
- In whatever form CAs are used to calculate results, CAs should be given in popular form, i.e., in weeks or months and weeks for the under 2-years-old and in years and months for the over 2-year-olds in reports.
- The reported results to be qualified as valid and reliable so that the reported finding may be considered acceptable.
- In cases where testing had to be abandoned or where results were only partial, incomplete, etc., no results can be permissible and only descriptive observation of the testing situation and the behaviour of the child may be given.
- Most importantly the report must always respond to the "reason for referral" and relate the final evaluation to it.

11 Some Memorable Moments During Assessments

Introduction

In the UK, the recognition in education of children with special needs is very recent as is the procedure for investigating and providing educational help to best meet the special needs child. In the old days, when slow developing children presented difficulties in the large mainstream classes of the time, they were assessed on tests of general mental development or intelligence. If their IQ was found to be outside the average range they were moved to special schools for the educationally subnormal. A majority of these children also presented health or behaviour problems and not infrequently were also seen in paediatric departments and child guidance clinics.

Motherly Love

It is in a paediatric setting that I first came across a little girl "R" and followed her up over many years.

"R" is now 11+ year old, still of a pleasant disposition with a round face and small eyes, which liven up with her frequent smiling. She continues to attend a special needs school.

"R's" Mother is a pleasant woman with apparent understanding of her daughter's slow mental development. "R" is the youngest of three, the other two, (a boy and a girl) are both in mainstream education and achieving very well. Mother has requested another assessment because she feels the school is not progressing "R's" attainments and her teachers also wish to have some advice to better structure "R's" educational programme.

During the course of the interview, Mother confides: "I know "R" may never grow up to be a rose, but perhaps she might get to be a lily". I find this floral metaphor, the product of a perception filtered through motherly love, somewhat touching and I echo a "perhaps who knows" in an impulsive response, then proceed to explain that after my assessment review of "R" I may be in a better position to offer practical and helpful advice on how best to meet "R's" scholastic needs.

I assess "R" without her mother present and predictably all goes smoothly. "R" cooperates as usual; she is by nature placid and conforming. We come to a verbal item that I had never used before with "R". It directs "R" to listen carefully to a short story. I state the instructions verbally out loud to her thus: "Listen. I am going to read out loud a short passage to you, and I want you to listen carefully because I am going to ask you questions about it afterwards." The short passage in question has a funny punch line at the end, which, if understood, should elicit some laughter.

Halfway through the story "R" bursts into fits of loud laughter.

"Why are you laughing," I query.

"Coz that's where my Mummy says I must laugh a lot," she replies simply and with a smile.

Mother had secured a copy of the test manual and coached "R" on this particular test item because it was the only one she thought "R" might be able to cope with and remember to give a correct response.

Shaken and Stirred

During a training session trainees are paired off to carry out hands-on practice. One of each pair is assigned as tester, "T"; the other as helper, "H". Each pair with child and parent are settled in an appropriate assessment room with a one-way observation window. Observers, "Os", are allocated their observation schedule. All seems to be set for a good start.

Unfortunately, works are being carried in the premises and soon noises and smells of paint become invasive, inducing stress. In addition, a couple of Os have missed their train connections and the observation schedules have to be altered. Os are now thin on the ground, resulting in discontinuous and inefficient observations.

In their room, T and H have started. "S" a six-year-old boy with speech problems, attending speech therapy classes, and his mother are seated side by side. Across the table T and H are observed engaged in a preamble conversation with mother and S in a relaxed way. The engagement process has started well.

The assessment proceeds; T is entirely focussed on correctly administrating test items and correctly assigning their scores. T goes methodically through every ordered sequence slowly and carefully while H sorts out the right pieces of test item or studies the instruction manual. Neither seems to look up from their tasks to look at either S and/or mother. This is not unusual with inexperienced trainees.

On my next observation, all seems in order. S is engaged on practical tasks.

Later T starts assessing S's verbal abilities. Seemingly unaware or unconcerned regarding the reported speech problem, T continues verbal testing despite a series of poor responses.

S finds verbal items increasingly difficult and begins to remain silent. Mother declares that she wishes to leave the room as she no longer wants to watch but both T and H explain that her presence is needed and S insists on his mother staying with him. Despite the increasing unease of S, who fails continuously, T perseveres with verbal tasks that are becoming quite difficult.

At this point I decide to intervene, and as I enter the room I see mother lashing out with her left arm towards S. There is a thumping noise; S has been thrown off his chair and is lying on the floor and mother is standing up in an agitated state sobbing and shouting, "I can't stand it any more." She turns to run out of the room, collides with me pinning me (for an instant) to the wall. We are now all standing up in the room in silence, dazed and shaken by the sudden distressing outburst. Within a split second, however, we stir and recover our self-control and start dealing with the situation.

Every time I recall this unusual session, I reflect at the power of feelings and emotions (which after all are the mental product of personally felt experiences) to display such an extraordinary surge of energy as to create havoc.

Finally Satisfied

One day a pregnant young woman attending the local antenatal clinic was asked by the health visitor whether she would agree to let her 2+-year-old "E" have a mental assessment for demonstration purposes as part of a professional training programme. The mother readily agreed. E was already attending nursery part-time.

They arrive punctually. Mother is charming, friendly and relaxed with a ready smile. The procedure is explained, and mother seems to understand that she should keep a low profile and not join in.

She immediately seats herself at the table opposite E saying quietly "If you don't mind, I'd like to watch." I find myself sitting in the middle with mother to one side and E to the other.

E proves cooperative with good verbal development. All goes well until E encounters a difficulty with a practical task. Mother dives in with a quiet sweet voice. Joining action to words explains: "No darling, no, watch, mummy do it for you. This goes here see, this one here, now I take it off and you put it back....well done."

I remind mother not to try and help her child and explain why.

We continue until the picture of a big orange and three different sized bowls item test, with the task of choosing the right size bowl for the orange, which E finds difficult. Yet again mother intervenes with, "Now darling, you can do that. Look this is the big orange, just like we have at home in the big bowl, and here look, here is the big bowl like the one at home. See. Now where shall we put the orange? The big bowl is here.... Yes, of course, in the big bowl like the one we have at home. Clever girl."

I remonstrate and remind her of the rules. Mother apologises, promising not to let it happen again, adding, "But it is hard because I know she can do it at home and at the nursery," all delivered in a gentle voice with her charming, friendly smile.

Because she is in an advanced stage of pregnancy, I do not wish to upset her. We proceed.

Mother intervenes once more in her usual manner and with a disarming smile turns to me to explain, "I do not want E to give the wrong impression and make the test seem no good; everyone must be allowed to see what my clever little E can do."

At this stage, I threaten to stop the testing, but she remonstrates, reminding me that it would be unfair to E if the assessment isn't completed. We complete the testing. Mother is pleased.

Strangely she does not ask about how well or otherwise her child has performed; instead she comments in her pleasant gentle way as follows: "I am very glad I was here with E to explain things clearly to her. You can't expect little children to understand your "la-dee-da" language. I know my little E is ever so clever and I am glad I was able to show it to you." She left apparently satisfied.

Epilogue

Beyond the Finishing Line: A Wide Angle Glance

This book has offered some glimpses into the complex nature of human mental development; into the two "faces" of psychology, and the psychological understanding of the multi-facetted functions of the mental process. It has looked into the ways that psychology as a science identifies and measures the dimensions of the mental process in development. The book has also stressed the nature and importance of the individual's felt experience.

Some effort has been made to show the limitations of individual tests of mental development and why learning to correctly administer and score a mental development test is necessary but not sufficient; why it requires of the user the ability to balance and blend quantitative findings with observed qualitative characteristics in a transient situation (a skill which is not easy to establish); and how the user can become inextricably entangled in the evaluation of a particular child in a particular situation at a point in time.

Throughout the book readers are reminded that both child and user have the same mental processing systems, but whereas the child is acquiring its style and biases and identity, those of the user's are already well established. Consequently, psychometric results of tests of mental development on their own as numerical values, valuable in themselves for research purpose and for epidemiological studies, are not sufficient to evaluate an individual child as a whole: an entity, a self adjusting organism, a human being with a thinking system not easily summed up by a series of discrete measurements of its displayed abilities. The emphasis is on the observation of the whole child within the child's total environment at a point in time.

In practice, therefore, a holistic approach is more likely to better serve the needs of the individual child. Indeed, the setting up of multi-disciplinary teams to assess the development of ability is spreading. Neuroscientists, neonatal paediatricians and psychologists are seen as the main contributors in the assessment process of identifying at risk needs in neonates and up to 2+-year-old infants and in setting up intervention programmes best suited to individual needs, which engage and support the family for as long as required. As yet, the issue of the mental assessment of the premature infant has not been considered.

Later, between the 3–8 years of age levels, the school is central to the life of the child. Within our society, any initial problems in the physics, chemistry and neurology of the individual child should have been already identified. While continued monitoring in these medical health areas remains necessary, it is teachers, psychologists and developmental paediatricians who appear to be better placed to note emergent difficulties in the learning process and in the displays of mental abilities of individual children. At this older age level, this group of professionals will be more suited to play a key role in the assessment of mental development and in the remediation programmes of individual need.

To the users and would be users who may have felt discouraged by the apparent complexity of mental assessment tasks, I offer the following quote from Antonio Damasio (2003), an expert neuroscientist, whose writings are pertinent to everyone engaged in the psychological evaluation of children's abilities. As humans we are constantly subject to "background emotional activities not especially prominent in one's behaviour, although they are remarkably important. You may never have paid much attention to it, but you are probably a good reader of background emotions if you accurately detect energy or enthusiasm in someone you have just met; or if you are capable of diagnosing some slight malaise or excitement, edginess or tranquillity, in your friends and colleagues. You assess the contour of movement in limbs and the whole body; How strong? How precise? How ample? How frequent? You observe facial expressions. If words do get uttered you do not just listen to the words and picture their dictionary meanings, you listen to the music in the voice, the prosody." (p. 43)

In short, when you assess an infant/child, as a competent observer you attend to the total situation, to the child in place and time, while you remain aware of your own "background emotions" for they are "remarkably important."

The user should heed the words of the oracle at Delphi ("Know thyself") before appraising mental development in others – knowing also implies the awareness of not knowing. To acquire knowledge from a master is nearly always much easier than trying to acquire knowledge from reading a book because it offers the possibility of an interactive exchange. To acquire knowledge by watching a task being done is even better as it provides sensory inputs from more than one modality. To acquire knowledge by becoming involved in a process, and experiencing it, is by far the best way to learn. This is why all training courses in the use of tests of mental ability for children should include hands on experience for their trainees, and all users should have a few test practice periods after first training to consolidate their learning.

As humans, we indeed constantly interact with our world and other humans in it and we evaluate situations almost automatically all the time. We do so naturally because this is the way our mental processing system functions: it reduces the seemingly chaotic input of stimuli from the world of realities into something simpler and understandable to ourselves. Basically, as humans, we seem to be born with the capacity to learn and to seek to resolve something not fully understood.

I leave you with "Me Daniel" (Preston, 1993) a poem about an 18-month-old, which illustrates how, like the little scientist that every child is, Daniel has to face the frustrations of finding that facts, sometimes, contradict the theory he has developed and how he learns through his experiences to take life in his stride.

"Unlike Adam and the forbidden fruit
Me Daniel eighteen months old
Needs not Eve or Serpent
Prompt him claim
The bauble on the Christmas tree
With the intense quiet of care
The shiny ball lined up
He targets his aim
The kick is hard and true
Yet no soaring vision sparks a path
For his eyes to follow through
Nothing but coloured tid-bits
Spread still about his feet
His glowing expectant face
Crumples tightly like tinfoil
Splattering sobs gut the silence

As Me Daniel starts
His descent from paradise

Me Daniel born eighteen months ago
In strange surrounds and gathering
Standing up and sizing up
Aware of cultural codes
Lets a tempting fruit rest outside his hold
Until the lady of the house voices
The sounds for yes or no

The sense of words bilingually he knows
Cats miaow, dogs woof-woof, a duck quack-quacks
But he cannot count. To him
All is one or the other – mostly the other

The finger thin buttered toast
Holds secret fascinations
Revealed only when halved
The cut releasing cascades of tears
Blinding and drowning the truth
One is one is all is one
His mother whispers soothing sounds
And as the dying tremors of his passion
Disperse into a last convulsion
He feeds her the dismembered pieces
Witness of a first kill.

Eighteen months old Me Daniel
With picture book on mother's lap
Discuss the order of dressing right
Animal life in the woods
Birds and things in the sky
An image, a colour, a sound stirs a memory
In language clear and fluent to them both
He recalls the bauble and the toast
Picture – deeds – and now a thought
One can be two – not all
Two can also be one – that's all

And of a sudden falls into sleep
To face another day
Crammed with discoveries
Gift wrapped with joy – bewilderment – and pain."
If "Me Daniel" can ....

Appendices

Appendix 1: How We Make Sense of Information Received: A Possible Model for the Structure of Thinking

The study of observed behaviour/performance/language displayed by infants and young children reveals a progressive organisation in the way received information is mentally processed and developed. It is represented below in the form of a possible model of the elements and structure of mental growth. Thus:

a) Sensory – Reception

All information captured through our sensory receptors from the external world of substance and through our sensory proprioceptors from the internal world of our bodily sensations are transmitted through neural pathways within our central nervous system. They appear to possess the qualities of attention, intention and exploration.

b) Perception

We perceive (recognise) sensory receptions as individually felt experiences of: shapes, colour, sounds, movement, and touch . These seem to simultaneously transmit affective qualities such as, for example, irritating/soothing, pleasant/unpleasant.

A range of apparently natural strategies get to work in some sort of sequential progression to enable us to make sense of all information received. At first, these appear to be automatic, subconsciously directed. All information is mentally processed; it is decoded, organised, synthesised, transformed. The final aim is to get to know, acquire knowledge, and use it to derive personal benefit according to need. This process appears to present progressive stages.

c) Stage I: Decoding

Identifying and recognising of objects, sounds, tastes, movements.

Noting differences and similarities

Sorting into groups
Organising into categories of shape, size, weight, volume, desirable, painful, etc
Transforming these into sets and subsets
Classifying
Differentiating degrees of loudness, silences, beats
Appreciating qualities of feelings
Developing an awareness of time, speed and space

In the first stages, the thinking mechanism appears to be at a concrete level in that it deals directly with the received information: the collected "raw data" is converted into a classified order.

d) Stage II: Evaluation

At this stage, the thinking mechanism tries to make sense out of classified data through processes such as:
Establishing constructs
Abstracting concepts
Making deductions
Formulating hypotheses
Engaging in predictions
Planning
Making formulations
Developing doubts/certainties

This stage is considered to be at the abstract level. It is abstract because it applies to the converted data; the direct sensory input is no longer critical to this stage of the mental process. It demonstrates the ability of the mental system to manipulate thinking in a way we call logical reasoning. (The blind from birth are capable of using mental processes of logical reasoning, Stage II, even though they will not have sensed visual input to structure Stage I decoding.)

e) Stage III: Resolution

This is a decision-making stage of applying the end results from the "trying to make sense" processes and strategies. The individual has reached the stage of knowing, of having made sense and needs to test out, apply or share this acquired knowledge. At this stage, the individual has a choice to disclose the knowledge or to keep it secret.

f) Stage IV: Action

A display pathway operates the interactive process of the resolution of the perceived individual experience and which, as a matter of choice, can be either revealed or retained in the private mental domain. Through the display pathways the overt (revealed) information is expressed through performance, behaviour, language. The individual interacts with the outside world and thereby brings about changes in the realities of the world and communicates with it. Overt information and/or its consequences get fed back to the sensory receptors as external realities and thereby become received information.

Covert information retained as a thought, a personal resolve, a dream, a vision may bring changes in the personal invisible mental perception but cannot bring about changes in the realities of the world, where it is unknown and has not interacted with it. Covert information forms an internal feedback to the mental thought process. It remains a secret.

g) Memory and Its Pathways

Memory is generally thought of as a storage system. It is not yet precisely known how and where memory is "stored," but it is clearly associated with certain areas in the brain. Memory pathways permit a retention and retrieval system mutually interactive in and with the mental processes at every stage. Its effectiveness determines the range and efficiency of the mental processing system. Memory and its pathways are not yet fully understood.

Appendix 2: Nature and Function of Measurement

I Measurement

Measurement means the assignment of numerals according to rules. One can distinguish four levels of measurements from the simplest to the more complex as follows:

Level a: The Nominal Scales. Here numbers are used to name, identify or classify. Numbers become mere labels, e.g., 1 = man, 2 = tree, 4 = bird.

The only arithmetical operation possible is:

1) Enumeration, e.g., four of 1, six of 2. Like oranges and apples, they can't be added together, multiplied, taken away or divided among themselves as this would be meaningless.

Level b: The Ordinal Scales. Here numbers indicate a rank order or series: 1st, 2nd, etc. They state a position. They enable comparisons, e.g., greater than or smaller than, or ahead of etc.

Arithmetical operations possible are:

1) Enumeration as above, and
2) Ranking methods and other statistical procedures based on interpretations of "greater than" or "less than."

Level c: The Interval Scales. The interval or distance between each number and the next is equal, but it is not known how far each is from the ZERO, e.g., thermometer readings, DQ and IQ test scores, etc., which are set from an chosen arbitrary zero point. Arithmetical operations possible are:

1) and 2) as above and

3) Addition and subtraction and statistical techniques based on these arithmetical operations.
4) Multiplication and division are not possible because they are meaningless, as, for example, in the case of IQ values: A child with an ability score of IQ120 cannot be said to have twice the ability of a child with an ability score of IQ60 and vice versa.

Level d: The Scalar Scales (Ratio Scale). Each number can be thought of as a distance measured form ZERO, e.g., the measurements of weight, lengths, time, etc. All arithmetical operations are possible:

1), 2), 3), and 4) multiplication and division. Scalar scales have the characteristics of:
interval scales plus the advantage of a true ZERO point.

A Few Things to Keep in Mind

The type of mathematics used varies according to the type of measurement required. Thus, measurements of temperature require the mathematics of an interval scale type. The mathematics for measuring quantities of weight or length require a scalar type. To measure direction one needs to assign signs, such as positive and negative loading to numbers. Zero as a numeral has peculiar properties, one of which is to define the concept of infinity in mathematical terms. In order to measure the distribution of a natural characteristic such as that of height, weight or mental ability, one requires the mathematics of the normal curve of frequency distribution.

In addition, it is necessary to remember that all measurements carried out by a human are subject to errors (mathematically known as errors of measurement: Em). These can be mathematically calculated. They are taken into consideration and allowances made accordingly when precision is needed.

II The Gaussian or Normal Frequency Distribution Curve

It is mostly psychologists who are interested in human characteristics. They study the distribution of human characteristics and their variations in individual cases. The most appropriate mathematical technique needed to measure any naturally occurring characteristic meaningfully is that of the frequency distribution, which naturally forms a bell-shaped curve. It applies only to very large samples.

Most of the tests psychologists work with are standardised tests, which are of the ordinal and interval variety and form a normal frequency distribution and which use the mathematics of the normal or "Gaussian" frequency distribution curve (so named after the mathematician who discovered its formula and properties). *The normal curve* shows a symmetrical distribution about its *mean* (the arithmetical average), which is also its *median* and its *mode*, and are measures of *convergence or centrality.* The median is the mid frequency value (it divides the distribution into equal halves); the mode is the most frequent value in the distribution. *Only in a normal distribution curve are these three values equal.* The base of the curve represents *the spread of the recorded observations set in rank order from lowest to highest recorded value.*

This variability of the frequency distribution can be calculated as a deviation from the mean called *standard deviation (SD or sigma). SD* is a measure of *spread* or *dispersion* (see figure below: “A model of the normal curve”), and it divides the base (range) into equal parts about its mean. Vertical elevations (frequency levels) drawn from these *SD* points to the curve *provide a measure of the percentage of frequencies within that portion of the curve.* In the normal curve, two thirds of all frequencies fall between the –1 SD and +1 SD values and the range spreads between –4 SD and +4 SD

Five main types of measurements are possible with any frequency curve distribution:

- i) *Centrality*, i.e., the position and value of the mean, the median and the mode
- ii) *Dispersion*, i.e., the size of the standard deviation or how distant a value is from the mean
- iii) *Range*, i.e., how wide apart is the lowest value from the highest
- iv) *Correlation*, i.e., the relationship between the values, i.e., bunched up or scattered about
- (v) *Significance*, i.e., probability of occurrence of the value, whether the value is likely or unlikely to be due to chance. Depending on the degree of precision demanded, a probability of occurrence less than 1 in 100 and up to less than 5 in 100 or $p = .05$ is usually accepted as significant, i.e., not likely to be due to chance.

III Scores

Not all measurements are scores: 5 meters of cloth is not a score; it is a measured length. Exams and games results, e.g., 5 out of ten or 2 out of 3, are scores. Scores are of two types:

1) *Raw scores* are the actual nominal values
2) *Standardised scores* are scores derived from a frequency distribution curve where the mean value and standard deviation have been

adjusted to comply with that of the normal frequency distribution curve.

IV Other Measurements

1) The Reliability of a test can be mathematically calculated through either the correlation coefficient or by using a special kind of standard deviation, namely the standard error (*SE*) measurement applied to the test. The *SE* is a guide to the general degree of inaccuracy one should allow for in interpreting scores and making decisions about individuals. For example, if the *SE* of an intelligence test is 5.00, there is a probability, of about two-thirds, that an individual's score is within 5.00 points of the score obtained: thus if an individual scores 130, his "true score" probably lies somewhere between 125 and 135. The probability of two thirds follows from the fact that in any normal distribution about two thirds of the scores fall within one standard deviation from the mean.

2) *Correlation* is measured by the coefficient of correlation. When measured values are bunched up (close to each other), they present a high correlation coefficient. If, on the other hand, they appear scattered (distant from each other), they present a low correlation. A correlation of +1 indicates complete interdependence, a correlation of –1 indicates complete opposition, and a 0 correlation indicates no interdependence. The correlation coefficient can also be used as a reliability coefficient of test re-test range, which is acceptable between +.75 and +.90.

3) *Validity* refers to the suitability of the test. A test is valid if it measures the characteristics it was designed to measure. Some tests may not be suitable for the purpose for which they are used, for instance, using a verbal test to tap the mental ability level of a child with severe speech problems, or using paper-and-pencil tasks to evaluate the mental ability of a partially sighted child. In both cases, the test results (if they are attempted at all) are useless and a waste of time.

4) *Significance* is calculated from the probability of occurrence of the value: whether the value is likely or unlikely to be due to chance. The error of measurement comes into the calculation. Depending on the degree of precision demanded, a probability of occurrence less than 1 in 100 and

up to and less than 5 in 100 or $p = .05$ is usually accepted as significant. If the calculated level of probability of occurrence of the difference between two recorded values falls between $p = .01$ and $p = .05$ then the difference is considered to be meaningful and not simply due to chance. A level of significance of $p = 0.05$ is usually accepted as being not due to chance.

Appendix 3: The Gaussian Curve and Equivalent Values

V The Normal Curve and Relationships Between some Types of Derived Scores

Figure 3a. The Normal Curve and relationships between some types of derived scores

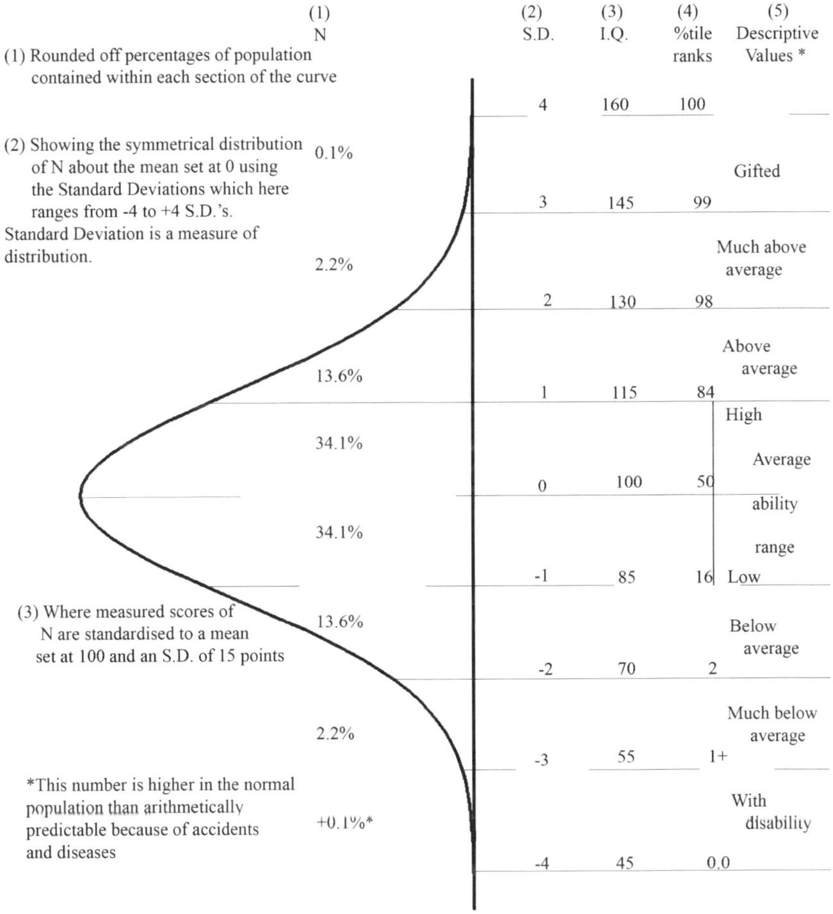

(4) Showing distribution as cumulative percentages. The majority clusters round the mean.

(5) The spread of N forms a continuum. Descriptive values overlap with their adjacent ranges.
* Descriptive values vary with social/political perception.

Appendix 4: Table of IQ Ranges and their *SD* Points and Descriptive Levels

IQ		SD points	Equivalent descriptive level
Expressed as a range			
1 *	>140	+4SD	Exceptionally high level of ability
2 *	130–139	+3SD	High level of ability
3	116–129	+2SD	Above average level of ability
4	106–115	+1SD	Good average level of ability
5	95–105	Mean (100) 0 SD	Average level of ability
6	85–94	–1SD	Low average level of ability
7 **	70–84	–2SD	Below average level of ability
8 **	55–69	–3SD	Much below average level of ability
9 **	< 54	–4SD	Exceptionally low level of ability

The numerical ranges (including error of measurement of +/– 5 points) are shown with their descriptive equivalents in current usage. The descriptive terms may alter from time to time according to the dictates of political correctness and cultural sensitivity. They apply to all tests of mental development where mental ability is translated as an IQ score as indicated above.

Note. * & ** have implications for health and special educational provisions.
For **, if required, consult the up-to-date WHO International Classification of Diseases for a more precise subgroup description of ranges of mental retardation.

Appendix 5: Notes on Play

It is inevitable and necessary for an infant to interact with his/her environment as this is the predominant means by which s/he can learn and develop.

There are different forms of interactions, but when a self determined activity is pursued from choice and for its own sake, it is called play.

At first the infant displays exploratory activities that provide him/her with some knowledge of some thing(s) in the environment. S/he also tries to imitate and then s/he initiates activities to practice this newly acquired knowledge. For example, let us consider a child handling a toy car:

a) First s/he may experience its weight, texture, shape, size, its qualities of rolling, its whirring sound when it moves or the spinning of the wheels, s/he may even taste and smell it, etc.
b) Later the infant is seen rolling the car gently or vigorously, chasing it, catching up with it, repeating this performance over and over again, apparently with enjoyment.
c) S/he may use two cars, race them, bump one against the other; s/he may be heard laughing at times.
d) S/he may dismantle it, break it up. Examine the pieces. Later s/he may attempt to reassemble it.

The infant is engaged in *play*, enjoying his growing knowledge of the toy car, and, through practice, establishes skills to control the car. Play feeds imagination and creativity.

Piaget's Noted Stages of Play

a) At first play is *imitative*; the infant/child appears to copy a piece of behaviour or a specific quality of something or someone; s/he does by examples; s/he tries to experience what it is to be a particular something or someone, e.g., helps tidy up, wash up, dust, etc.
b) Then comes *exploratory play*, which is followed or is simultaneous with
c) practice or *mastery play* as explained in above examples.
d) Not uncommonly, the child acts as if s/he is a car, a king, an animal, etc. This is a make belief form of play, which persists through to adulthood. It is called *pretend play*. A child would say "Pre-

tend –, I am the teacher, – Pretend the toys can talk, make them talk – Pretend I am a baby."

e) Much later play becomes *symbolic*. At this advanced stage, the use of objects or designs stand in as identifiers to indicate specific groups such as, for example, pictures of various animals to represent various gangs in play acting, or a picture of objects to indicate a trade or craft, or a logo to express a concept (e.g., in our culture the dove and/or the olive branch represents "peace").

By and by play becomes structured, it acquires rules, it becomes games, and as such applies to adults too. Usually games, or "play by rules," are social events. They demand participation with others (except nowadays with computer games, which are often played solo).

Games demand consensus, an agreement to abide by rules and sometimes to concede to the wishes of a leader; they have a social dimension.

Play as the "unconscious self" expressed. This leads to the assumption that what a child does in free play may reflect or reveal unconscious (i.e., not expressed) wishes and feelings, such as fears; an assumption which has led to the use of *play as a tool of therapies* with children.

Appendix 6: Language Development

A Summary

The development of language acquisition in the infant has been extensively studied by psychologists and psycholinguists. By now it is established that even before birth the human embryo, in its fifth month, responds to the spoken voice. A recent book by Bénédicte de Boysson-Bardies "How language comes to children" reveals that from the moment of birth on the human infant enters into a dialogue with his/her world (i.e., his/her mother at first then his/her environment), and proceeds through listening, sorting, selecting, ordering and structuring sounds to establish an understanding of language before the physical maturation which enables the articulation of speech. It would appear that the role of the mother-infant baby talk interaction, or "motherese," is crucial to this learning process because it captures the attention of the baby, motivates exchanges, and provides melodic intonations which convey affective values. Bénédicte de Boysson-Bardies's careful observation show that the human infant, "with all the limitations of an immature neuro/central nervous system, deploys from birth evidence of sensory discrimination and expressive emotive capacity, coloured by individual styling, which leads her to conclude that the human infant's ability to acquire language is genetically based.

Psychologists and psycholinguists have examined the element of the genetically based mental technology which underlies all language systems as divulged by the child. Their conclusions are thought provoking mainly because this natural technology – somewhat unconsciously operated – is human specific, and it is through speech/language that we structure our world.

This author's approach to her work is similar to that of the late Ruth Griffiths, in that they both derive their material from direct observation of the child in interaction with his/her world. However, there is a fundamental difference between them. Ruth Griffiths looks at the "whole": moods, qualities of attention and listening, social interactive style etc. Thus, in the 0–2 year range of the Griffiths Scale, the test item "responds to name" demonstrates the recognition of a mental process, acquired knowledge, the understanding of the concept "name," the recognition of a word/sound specific in relation to the child (an awareness of one's self) as well as listening functions.

Included here below (Part B)is a translation of de Boysson-Bardies's table summary of the stages of language development from 0–2 years (pp. 247–249 in the original book). Her detailed progression of speech/language development shows a high degree of correspondence with Ruth Griffith's language stages, which is quite remarkable given the time gap between the two studies and the different languages and cultures that the sampled populations studied.

B. Table Showing in Summary the Developmental Stages of Speech in Infancy: 0–2

Speech/Language Perception	Speech/Language Expression
1. Pre-birth – Reaction to spoken voice – Preference for maternal voice – Discrimination between sounds	– Recorded changes in the natural rhythms breathing, heart beats etc. of the foetus to sounds
2. Birth to 1 month – Continued discrimination and preference for the maternal voice – Sensitivity to rhythm, tone and style of speech, i.e., prosody	– Cries, tears, vegetative sounds – Sounds of discomfort/unease
3. From 1 to 5 months – Able to categorise sounds despite variable intonation – Recognises one syllable in differing enunciation – Detects changes in the schema of intonations – Appearance of controlled phonation	– First laughter, small cries of joy – Vocalises opening and closing mouth – First "arrh" with glottal sounds
4. From 5 to 7 months – Preference for the "Motherese" – Categorisation of vowels according to mother tongue – Detects the prosody form (varies in different languages) – Experiments with mouthing vowel sounds	– Controlled vocalisations – Plays games with intonations – Variations and imitations – Starts to babble with consonants, alternating rhythmically

5. From 7 to 10 months – Preference for words of constant stress and constraints of native language – Able to recognise words in phrases after training – Differences appear in the babbling of infants – Starts to understand words in context according to the linguistic environment	– Production of vowels akin to mother tongue – Babbles with varied sequences of syllables – Shapes intonation according to mother tongue in these words
6. From 10 to 12 months – Detects the frontiers of words – Reorganises perceptual categories according to the phonological structure of the mother tongue – Recognises known words out of context – Understands about 30 words in context – Learns words by association to a reference	– Selects a repertory of vowels and consonants – Adapted to the mother tongue – Babbles in sequences of varied length and intonation – Emergence of stable pattern of expression in relation to situations
7. From 12 to 16 months – Understands on average 100 to 150 words – Understands the idea of phrases and simple phrases	– Babble persists with phrase like intonations – Forms more consistent expressive patterns in relation to situations – Utters on average 50 words, mostly nouns – Exhibits different styles of entry into the language
8. From 16 to 20 months – Understands on average 200 words – Can distinguish categories in words	– Can produce between 50 and 170 words – Increased production of verbs and verbal expressions

9. From 20 to 24 months	
– Understands relations – Understands the syntax of words provided that context, semantics and prosody are coherent	– Rapid growth of vocabulary – Some can achieve up to 300 words – Reorganises the pronunciation of words – Prepares a phonological lexicon – Makes 2/3 word phrases, few articles yet but starts acquisition of gender and number

Some Additional Interesting Information

Infants as young as 20 months differentiate between "gone" and "finished," i.e., between a person/object out of sight and which may not reappear, and a process (e.g. a piece of music or story) which has come to an end but which could be restarted (see pp. 237–238 of the original book).

Appendix 7: The Hand
(Notes derived from the book "Touching for Knowing" by Hatwell, Streri, & Gentaz, 2003)

The overwhelming evidence of vision as the most important of the senses to learning and the acquisition of knowledge has overshadowed the role of the hand as a sensory organ. Although complementary to vision in many instances, touch does provide essential and additional sensory information in its own right.

The hand, with its arm and shoulder support, is observed in the GMD Infant scales and noted mainly in the developmental stages of grasp, reach, hold, etc., and in the hand-eye co-ordination tasks.

As a fine instrument of exploration, the hand is also noted in the GMDS and BSID II: items such as "scratches, as if to feel the surface of the table" and later in judging "the heavy one" in the weight test (GMDS 2+–8 extension), and also as an instrument of precision in threading, drawing, etc.

The fingers as well as the palm are very sensitive and together they provide the infant/child with information as to shape, size, weight, texture, depth, volume, soft/hard, temperature, etc., which the eye alone cannot impart.

Consider for a moment the additional information derived by not just looking at a sculpture/a painting/an object, but by exploring it with the hands as well. Through stroking movements, static contact, applied pressure, lifting, grasping, following contours with finger, pinching, sinking into, etc., the appreciation of texture, temperature, thickness, weight, volume, shape and hidden depths, etc. are conveyed. The hand adds different modalities to visual perception.

A recent book "Toucher pour Connaître" (2002) by a group of cognitive psychologists and edited by psychologist Prof. Y. Hatwell, now in its English translation "Touching for Knowing" (2003), presents a psychological study of the sensory function of the hand, its localised cortical representation, and the sensory pathways it helps structure. The book covers the following areas:

a) The anatomical and neurological basis underlying tactile perceptions of the hand and their perceptual organisational representation in the cortex.
b) The variety and extent of its exploratory information seeking activities.

c) Its tactile functions in relation to vision (directed or not) and their role in structuring memory. There is also an interesting chapter on the perceptive tactile exploration in non-human primates.
d) The formation of resultant spatial imageries and their relation with linguistic representations.
e) Modality – inter, mixed, transfers of, preferential etc., hand eye co-ordination in the child and the adult, hand dominance and laterality.
f) Lastly, but importantly, the book also discusses some derived practical applications helpful to the visually impaired, an area of particular interest to Prof. Hatwell and to which she has made many contributions.

It would appear that the hand provides essential sensory inputs that complement all sensory derived inputs (the visual, auditory, gustatory, etc.) and thereby restructures the perception of the information received from them. The GMDS, GMDS (ER) and BSID II help plot this process in development.

The following illustration, Figure 7a, shows that while the hands of the Higher Anthropoid Apes and those of the Homos are very similar in structure, the humans have shown a remarkably greater control over a finer and wider range of hand/finger movements. This may be due to a more developed brain in the humans arising from their need to use their hands/fingers in more varied ways more often.

Figure 7a. Illustration of the palmar view of the right hands of Primates an Homo (from A.H. Schult and R.D. Martin)

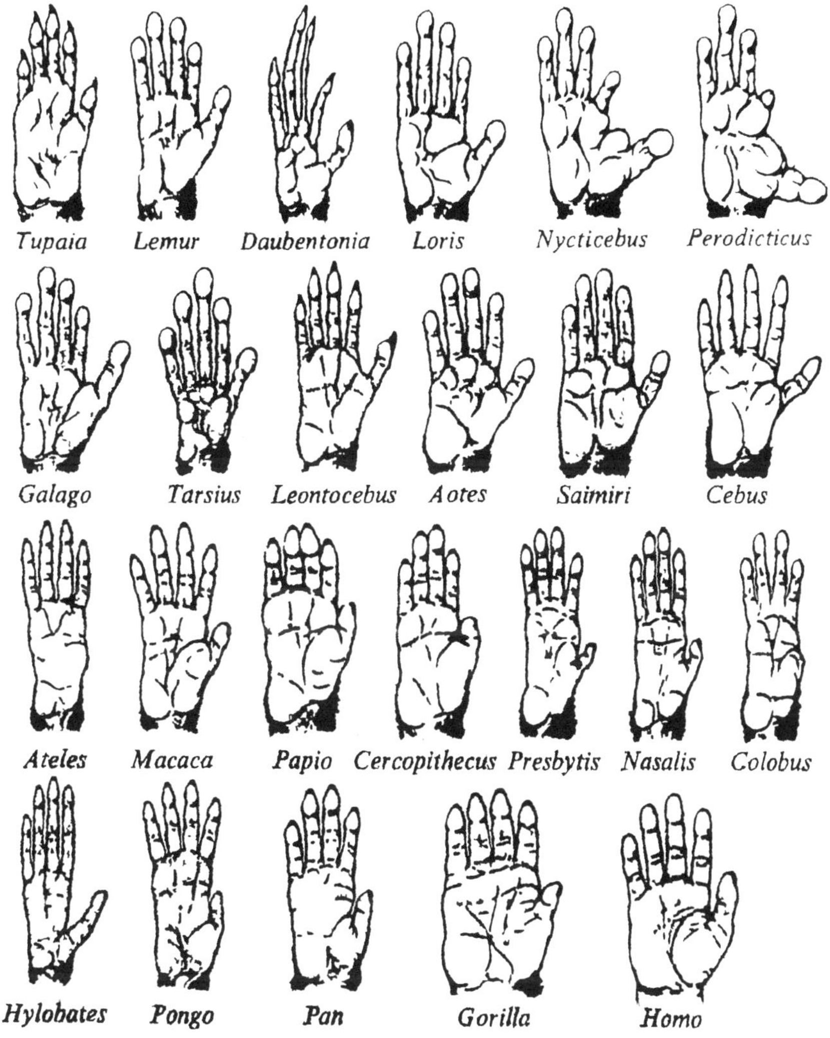

(i) Tupaia – Tarsius: Prosimians no longer classifieed in the primates category
(ii) Leontocebus – Ateles: New World monkeys
(iii) Macaca-Colobus: Old World monkeys
(iv) Hylobates-Gorilla: Anthropoid apes
(v) Homo

Figure 7b. Hand Function (after Halverson)

showing the trend in the development of grasping for an object to move distally and radially with respect to the palm, as follows:

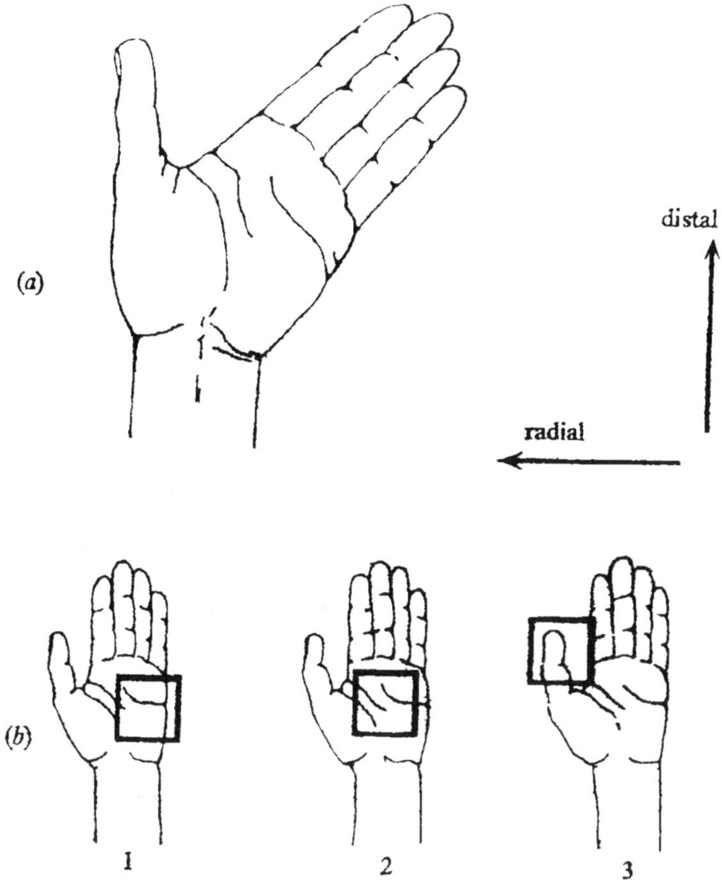

stage (a) Human hand showing ulnar deviation

stage (b) Position of a cube relative to the palm, showing radial an distal shift position with increasing age: 1. 15 weeks; 2. 24 weeks; 3. 36 weeks

Figure 7c. Prehension (after Napier, 1961) – Diagrammatic representation of human thumb opposition

Opposition occurs only when abduction and rotation are combined with flexion. Abduction and rotation, or flexion alone, do not achieve opposition.

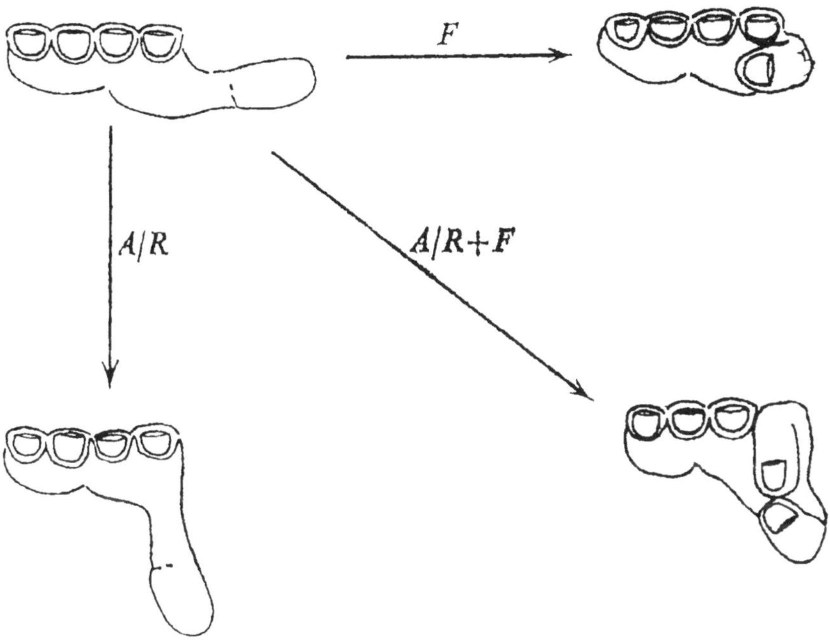

A/R = abduction and rotation
F = flexion
A/R + F = fine prehension; thumb opposition complete

Figure 7d. Developmental Stages in the 'reach' in early infancy – after Halverson (1943)

Diagrammatic representation of progressive reduction in lateral deviation of hand (and arm) of human infant reaching for a cube. The obvserved vertical 'loop' movement is gradually replaced by a horizontal sliding fluent movement which targets the cube.

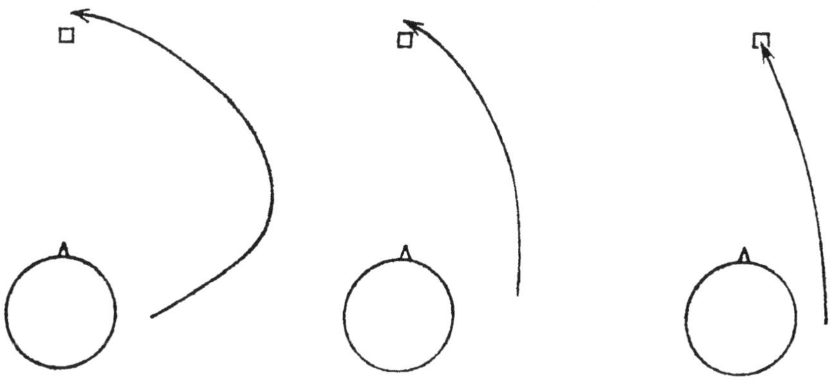

(*a*) at 28 weeks

(*b*) at 36 weeks

(*c*) at 52 weeks

Appendix 8: Facial Expressions

Figure 8a. Illustration diagram of mouth structure – after L. Humphries (1969)

Some examples of interaction in the form of mouth units.

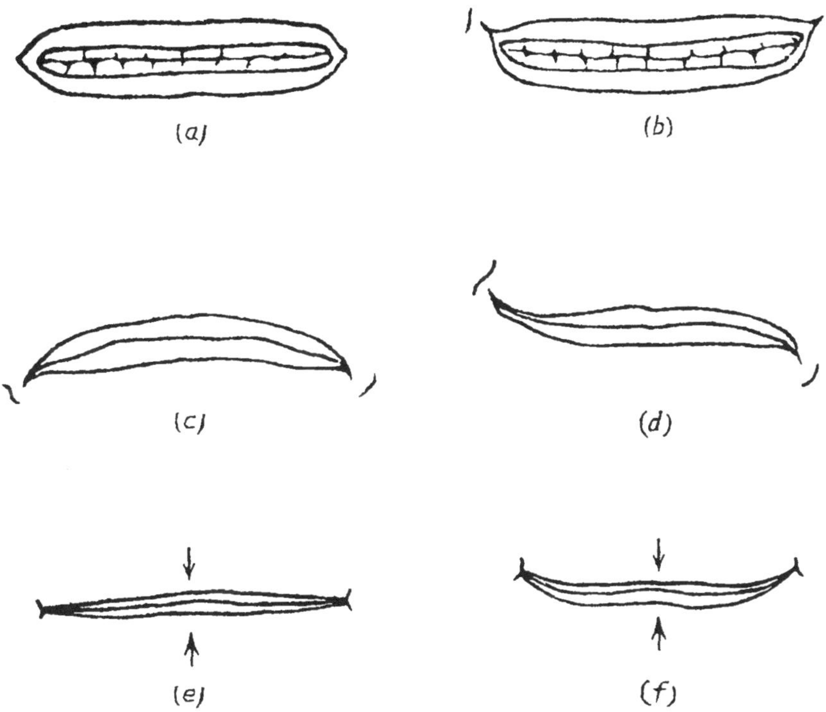

(a) oblong mouth
(b) oblong 'smile'
(c) 'mouth corner down'
(d) wry smile
(e) tight lips
(f) compressed lips

Figure 8b. Illustration diagram of facial expressions – after L. Humphries (1969)

Combination of elements of facial structure appear to be symmetrical and involve different, often subtly so, aspects of facial structure.

(a) (b) eye region and mouth region both indicate affect states
(c) (d) overall impression of affect alters when 'mouth corners down' is combined with different 'frowns'
(e) (f) similarly – illustration of antithesis of smile and 'mouth corners down' structure

References

Bayley, N. (1993). *Bayley Scales of Infant Development: Second Edition.* San Antonio, TX: Harcourt Assessment, Inc.

Binet, A., & Simon, T. (1905). Méthodes nouvelles pour le diagnostic du niveau intellectuel des anormaux [New methods for the diagnosis of the intellectual level of subnormals]. *L'Année psychologique, 11,* 191–244.

Clarke, A. D. B., & Clarke, A. M. (1973). *Mental retardation and behaviourial research.* Edinburgh, UK: Churchill Livingston.

Cocteau, J. (1953/2003). *Journal d'un inconnu.* Paris:Grasset.

Boysson Bardies, B. (2004). *Comment la parole vient aux enfants* [How children develop language]. (Arlette Steri & Edawr Genta, trans.). Paris: Edile Jacob.

Damasio, A. (2003). *Looking for Spinoza: Joy, sorrow and the feeling brain*. New York: Harcourt.

Edelman, G. M., & Mountcastle, V. B. (Eds.) (1978). *The mindful brain: Cortical organization and the group selective theory of higher brain functions.* London: MIT Press.

Faragher, B. (in press). *Update conversion data tables in GMDS-ER Technical Manual.* Oxford, UK: The Test Agency Ltd.

Freeman, W. J. (1999). *How brains make up their minds.* London: Weidenfeld & Nicolson.

Gardner, H. (1993a). Multiple intelligences: The theory in practice. New York: Basic Books.

Gardner, H. (1 993b). Creating minds. New York: Basic Books.

Gesell, A. (1925). The mental growth of the pre-school child: A psychological outline of normal development from birth to the sixth year including a system of developmental diagnosis. New York: Cornell University.

Goodenough, F. (1926). A new approach to the measurement of intelligence of young children. *Journal of Genetic Psychology, 33,* 185–211.

Griffiths, R. (1935). A study of imagination in early childhood and its function in mental development. London: K. Paul, Trench, Trubner.

Griffiths R. (1954). *The abilities of babies: Griffiths Mental Devleopment Scales (GMDS) 0-2 years*. London: University of London Press.

Griffiths R. (1970). *The abilities of young children: Griffiths Mental Devleopment Scales (GMDS) Extension 2–8 yrs. A study in mental measurement*. Oxford, UK: The Test Agency.

Griffiths, R. (1996 revision by Huntley, M). The Griffiths Mental Development Scales (GMDS) 0-2 years revision. Oxford, UK: The Test Agency.

Hatwell, Y. (2003a). *Psychologie cognitive de la cécité précoce* [Cognitive Psychology of early blindness]. Paris: Dunod.

Hatwell, Y., Streri, A., & Gentaz, E. (Eds.) (2003b). *Touching for knowing: Cognitive psychology of haptic manual perception*. Amsterdam & Philadelphia: John Benjamin Publishers.

Holt, K., & Reynell, J. J. (1970). *Observation of children*. London: NAMH publication.

Keats, J. (1884). 37. Lamia: Part II. In J. Keats, *Poetical works*. London: Macmillan.

Koffka, K. (1935). *Principles of Gestalt Psychology*. New York: Harcourt & Brace.

Piaget, J. (1936/1952). The origin of intelligence in the child. New York: Basic Books.

Piaget, J. (1937/1954). The construction of reality in the child. New York: International University Press.

Piaget, J., & Inhelder, B. (1947/1967). The child's conception of space. New York: W. W. Norton

Preston, P. (1993). *Developmental Sketches: 0–4 Psychology in Verse*. Unpublished poetry collection.

Proust, M. (1982). *Remembrance of things past* (pp. 48–51). (C.K. Scott Moncrieff & T. Kilmartin, Trans.). New York: Vintage.

Romanyshyn, R. D. (1982). *Psychological life: From science to metaphor*. Austin, TX: University of Texas Press.

Sheldrake, R. (2003). *The sense of being stared at and other aspects of the extended mind*. London: Hutchinson.

Spearman, C. (1904). "General intelligence," objectively determined and measured. *American Journal of Psychology, 15*, 201–293.

Stutsman, R. (1931). Merrill-Palmer Scale of Mental Tests. Chicago: Stoelting Co.

Terman, L. M. (1916). *The measurement of intelligence: An explanation of and a complete guide for the Stanford revision and extension of the Binet-Simon Scale*. Boston: Houghton Mifflin.

Terman, L. M. (1972 UK version). The Stanford-Binet Intelligence Scale Manual (3rd rev.). London: Harraps & Co. Ltd.

The Education Act 1970. London: HMSO.

Varela, F.J., Thompson, E., & Rosch, E. (1991) *The embodied mind: Cognitive science and human experience*. Cambridge, MA: The MIT Press.

Warren, D. H. (1984). *Blindness and early childhood development* (2nd ed.). New York: American Foundation for the Blind.

Wechsler, D. (1976). *Wechsler Intelligence Scale for Children: Revised British Amendments*. London: NFER Publishing.

Wechsler, D. & Rust, J. (UK project Director). (2003). *Wechsler Preschool and Primary Scale of Intelligence – UK Edition* (WPPSI-III UK). London: Harcourt Assessment.